WAR AND THE TRANSFORMATION OF BRITISH SOCIETY 1931–1951

GCSE Modern World History for Edexcel

Steve Waugh
John Wright

The Publishers would like to thank the following for permission to reproduce copyright material:

Photo credits
pp.4, 15, 18, 25 *b*, 28, 32 *l*, **p.52** *l*, 61 *both*, 91 *b* Hulton Archive/Getty Images; **pp.8** *l*, 54 *b* Getty Images; **pp.8**, 48, 51, 55, 73 © Bettmann/CORBIS; **p.10** Gateshead Council; **p.11** Express Syndication/*Daily Express*; **pp.19**, 27, 49, 53 *l*, 64 Popperfoto/Getty Images; **p.21** Travel Ink/Getty Images; **pp.25** *t*, 41, 52 *r*, 53 *r*, 62 *b*, 67, 104 © Hulton-Deutsch Collection/CORBIS; **pp.30**, 83, 106 © Trinity Mirror/Mirrorpix/Alamy; **pp.31**, 78 Solo Syndication/The British Cartoon Archive, University of Kent; **p.32** *r* Library of Congress; **p.34** AP/PA Photos; **pp.36**, 95, 97 *t*, 99, 109 Solo Syndication/*London Evening Standard*/The British Cartoon Archive, University of Kent; **pp.43**, 82 *t* © Photos 12/Alamy; **p.44** © David Pollack/CORBIS; **p.45** The Granger Collection/TopFoto; **pp.47**, 63 *l*, 75 The National Archives/HIP/TopFoto; **p.54** *t*, 87 Time & Life Pictures/Getty Images; **pp.58**, 63 *r*, 71, 72 Public Record Office/HIP/TopFoto; **pp.59**, 79 *l* Imperial War Museum Photo Archive; **pp.60**, 107 TopFoto; **p.62** *t* Reg Speller/Fox Photos/Hulton Archive/Getty Images; **p.65** Ealing/The Kobal Collection; **p.79** *r* Courtesy of New Orleans Public Library; **p.80** Three Lions/Getty Images; **p.82** *b* Solo Syndication/Llyfrgell Genedlaethol Cymru/National Library of Wales; **pp.88**, 101 Solo Syndication/*Daily Mail*/British Cartoon Archive, University of Kent; **p.91** *t* Picturepoint/Topfoto; **p.92** The Granger Collection/Topfoto; **p.97** *b* Daily Mirror Newspapers/Mirrorpix; **p.108** Punch Limited/TopFoto; **pp.110**, 111 Express Syndication/*Daily Express*/British Cartoon Archive, University of Kent.

Acknowledgements
p.3 Edexel Limited, *History A: The Making of the Modern World*, 2209; **p.5** P. Sauvain, *Key Themes of the Twentieth Century*, Nelson Thornes, 1996; **p.7** J. Brooman, *The Era of the Second World War*, Longman, 1993; **p.9** N. DeMarco and R. Radway, *The Twentieth Century World*, Nelson Thornes, 1995; **p.10** S. Constantine, *Unemployment in Britain Between the Wars*, Longman, 1980; **pp.12** A, 16 *both* C. Culpin, *The People's Century*, Collins Educational, 1994; **p.12** B J. Stevenson and C. Cook, *Britain in the Depression*, Longman, 1994; **pp.13**, 14, 19, 22, 23 C, 50 H, J, 53, 56 B, 76 B S. Waugh, *Essential Modern World History*, Nelson Thornes, 2001; **pp.15** C, 17 C George Orwell, *The Road to Wigan Pier*, Victor Gollancz, 1937; **pp.15** D, 24, 26 A B. O'Callaghan, *A History of the Twentieth Century*, Longman, 1987; **pp.17** D, 18, 23 F, 25, 104 C J. Brooman, *People in Change*, Longman, 1994; **pp.23** D, E, 24 B, C J. D. Clare, *The Twentieth Century*, Nelson Thornes, 1999; **p.26** B Jonathan Glancey and Peter Hetherington, *Guardian*, 18 September 2003; **p.26** C D. Ferriby and J. McCabe, *Modern Word History for AQA*, Heinemann, 2001; **p.26** D BBC Tyne Features, 'The March to Jarrow'; **p.27** S. N. Broadberry, *The British Economy Between the Wars*, Blackwell, 1986; **pp.29**, 37 A Clive Pointing, *1940: Myth and Reality*, Cardinal Books, 1990; **pp.32**, 35 C House of Commons; **p.34** A *Daily Mail*, 1 June 1940; **p.37** *New York Times*, 1 June 1940; **pp.40**, 41 C. K. MacDonald, *The Second World War*, Simon & Schuster Education, 1984; **pp.43** A, 50 G, 56 C B. Walsh, *Modern World History*, Murray, 1996; **p.43** B L. Deighton, *Fighter*, Jonathan Cape, 1977; **p.44** National Library of Scotland; **p.45** A, C *Images of War Volume 2*, Imperial War Museum, 1993; **p.48** C *Daily Herald*, 16 November 1940; **p.50** F, I M. Chandler, *Britain in the Age of Total War 1939–45*, Heinemann, 2002; **p.54** F. Reynoldson, *War at Home*, Heinemann, 1980; **pp.55**, 74 F N. DeMarco, *The Second World War*, Hodder, 1997; **p.63** www.johndclare.net; **p.67** S. Briggs, *Keep Smiling Through*, Weidenfeld & Nicolson, 1975; **p.69** Paul Addison, *The Road to 1945*, Pimlico, 1994; **p.70** B E. Roosevelt, *The Autobiography of Eleanor Roosevelt*, HarperCollins, 1961; **p.70** C J. Croall, *Don't You Know There's a War On?*, Random House, 1989; **pp.71**, 74 C, D, E R. Minns, *Bombers & Mash*, Virago Press, 1980; **p.77** Laurent Lefebvre, *They Were on Omaha Beach*, American D-Day, 2004; **p.85** J. Laver, *The Modernisation of Russia 1856–1985*, Heinemann, 2002; **pp.89**, 94 B, 104 E, 110 B P. Hennessy, *Never Again: Britain 1945–51*, Jonathan Cape, 1992; **p.94** C H. Macmillan, *Tides of Fortune*, Harper & Row, 1969; **p.94** D bbc.co.uk; **p.97** C H. Morrison, *An Autobiography*, Odhams Press Ltd, 1960; **p.101** *Picture Post*, February 1943; **p.104** D P. J. Madgwick, *Britain Since 1945*, Nelson Thornes, 1982; **pp.105** A, B, 106, 111 E N. Timmins, *The Five Giants*, HarperCollins, 1995; **p.109** *Daily Sketch*, February 1948; **p.110** A *Daily Mail*, 3 July 1948.

Every effort has been made to trace all copyright holders, but if any have been inadvertently overlooked the Publishers will be pleased to make the necessary arrangements at the first opportunity.

Although every effort has been made to ensure that website addresses are correct at time of going to press, Hodder Education cannot be held responsible for the content of any website mentioned in this book. It is sometimes possible to find a relocated web page by typing in the address of the home page for a website in the URL window of your browser.

Orders: please contact Bookpoint Ltd, 130 Milton Park, Abingdon, Oxon OX14 4SB. Telephone: (44) 01235 827720. Fax: (44) 01235 400454. Lines are open 9.00 – 5.00, Monday to Saturday, with a 24-hour message answering service. Visit our website at www.hoddereducation.co.uk

First published in 2010 by
Hodder Education,
An Hachette UK company
338 Euston Road
London NW1 3BH

Impression number   5 4 3 2
Year   2014 2013 2012

Edited and designed by White-Thomson Publishing www.wtpub.co.uk
Clare Collinson (editorial); Amy Sparks and Simon Borrough (design).

Cover photos *l* © Bettmann/CORBIS, *r* Savill/Getty Images

Printed in Dubai

A catalogue record for this title is available from the British Library.
ISBN: 978-0-340-98435-2

Contents

Introduction

About the course

During this course you must study four units:

- **Unit 1** Peace and War: International Relations 1900–1991
- **Unit 2** Modern World Depth Study
- **Unit 3** Modern World Source Enquiry
- **Unit 4** Representations of History.

These units are assessed through three examination papers and one controlled assessment:

- In Unit 1 you have one hour and 15 minutes to answer questions on three different topics from International Relations 1900–1991.
- In Unit 2 you have one hour and 15 minutes to answer questions on a Modern World Depth Study.
- In Unit 3 you have one hour and 15 minutes to answer source questions on one Modern World Source Enquiry topic.
- In the controlled assessment you have to complete a task under controlled conditions in the classroom (Unit 4).

About the book

This book has been written to support option 3B 'War and the transformation of British society *c.*1931–51' in Unit 3. It covers the key developments in Britain from 1931 to 1951 through four key topics, each with three chapters:

- **Key Topic 1** examines the impact of the Depression 1931–39, looking at the growth of unemployment and the government response, the experience of the unemployed and the key features of the Jarrow Crusade.
- **Key Topic 2** examines Britain's experience in the Second World War. It looks at the part played by the British Expeditionary Force (BEF) in France and Belgium, including the significance of the Dunkirk evacuation and role of Churchill, the Battle of Britain and the effects of the Blitz.

- **Key Topic 3** also looks at Britain at war. It examines the increased role of government on the home front, including the impact of rationing of food, the changing role of women brought about by their contribution to the war, and the part played by the British in the D-Day landings and the subsequent advance on Germany.
- **Key Topic 4** looks at the post-war period when the Labour Party was in power, 1945–51. It examines the Labour Party election victory of 1945 and the subsequent creation of a welfare state including National Insurance and the setting up of the National Health Service.

Each chapter in this book:

- contains activities – some develop the historical skills you will need, others are exam-style questions that give you the opportunity to practise exam skills. The exam-style questions are highlighted in green.
- gives step-by-step guidance, model answers and advice on how to answer particular question types in Unit 3.
- highlights glossary terms in bold the first time they appear in each key topic.

About Unit 3

Unit 3 is a test of:

- the ability to answer a range of source questions
- knowledge and understanding of the key developments in each of the four key topics.

The examination paper will include five or six sources, including:

- written sources, such as extracts from diaries, speeches, letters, poems, songs, biographies, autobiographies, memoirs, newspapers, modern history textbooks and the views of historians
- illustrations, such as photographs, posters, cartoons or paintings.

Below is a set of specimen questions (without the sources). You will be given step-by-step guidance throughout the book on how best to approach and answer these types of questions.

This is an **inference** question. You have to get a message or messages from the source.

This is a **source interpretation** question, asking you to explain the purpose of the source – why it was produced. This question could also be phrased as:
- Why was this newspaper article published?

This is a **cross-referencing** question. It is asking you to compare the views of the three sources and explain whether or not they support the view given in the question. This question could also be phrased as:
- Do these sources support the view that …?
- Do Sources A and B support the view of Source C that …?
- How far do Sources A and B support the view of Source C about …?

This is a **reliability** question. It is asking you to decide how reliable each source is. This could also be a **utility** question, where you must decide how useful each source is.

This is a **hypothesis testing** question. It is asking you to use the sources and your own knowledge to test a hypothesis.

1. Study Source A.
What can you learn from Source A about the German bombing raid on Coventry?

(6 marks)

2. Study Source C and use your own knowledge.
What was the purpose of this newspaper article? Use details from the article and your own knowledge to explain your answer.

(8 marks)

3. Study Sources A, B, and C.
How far do these sources agree about the German bombing of Coventry, November 1940? Explain your answer, using the sources.

(10 marks)

4. Study Sources D and E.
How reliable are Sources D and E as evidence of the German Blitz of 1940–41? Explain your answer, using Sources D and E and your own knowledge.

(10 marks)

5. Study all the sources and use your own knowledge.

'Lowering the morale of the British people was the worst effect of the Blitz.'

How far do the sources in this paper support this statement? Use details from the sources and your own knowledge to explain your answer.

(16 marks)

(Total 50 marks)

Key Topic 1: The impact of the Depression 1931–39

Tasks

1. *Look at Source A. What message is the photographer trying to put across?*

2. *How does the photographer achieve this?*

From 1929, directly as a result of the **Wall Street Crash**, Britain experienced a **depression**, which in turn brought high unemployment. By 1932, nearly one worker in four was out of a job. Certain areas of Britain, known as the 'Depressed Areas' or 'Special Areas', were badly affected. The government brought in a series of measures to deal with unemployment, including the infamous Means Test. The unemployed responded with a series of hunger marches, the most famous of which was the **Jarrow Crusade** of 1936.

Each chapter explains a key issue and examines important lines of enquiry as outlined below.

Chapter 1: The growth of unemployment and the government response (pages 5–12)
- Why was unemployment so high in certain areas?
- What measures were brought in by the government to deal with unemployment?

Chapter 2: The experience of the unemployed (pages 13–20)
- Why was the Means Test so unpopular?
- What effects did unemployment have on the standard of living?

Chapter 3: The Jarrow Crusade (pages 21–27)
- Why was the Jarrow March organised?
- What happened during the Jarrow March?
- What did the Jarrow March achieve?

The growth of unemployment and the government response

Task

Study Source A. What can you learn from Source A about unemployment in the 1930s? (For guidance on answering this type of question, see page 12.)

Britain experienced high unemployment in the 1930s. This was partly due to longer term weaknesses in the British economy, especially the over-reliance on declining heavy industries such as iron and steel, coal, shipbuilding and cotton, but it was also due to the repercussions of the Wall Street Crash. Government attempts to deal with unemployment were not very effective and in some cases made the situation worse.

This chapter answers the following questions:

• Why was unemployment so high in certain areas?
• What measures were brought in by the government to deal with unemployment?

Examination skills

In this chapter you will be given guidance on how to answer the inference question, which is worth six marks.

Why was unemployment so high in certain areas?

On 29 October 1929 Wall Street, the US stock exchange, collapsed. Hundreds of thousands of people lost their life savings. Banks collapsed because loans were not repaid. Businesses went bust as people stopped buying goods, and the **Great Depression** began, which caused very high unemployment. The USA could no longer afford to lend money to European countries and recalled some of its earlier loans. Therefore economic depression soon hit Britain and the rest of Europe because of their over-dependence on the USA.

In Britain, the main effect was caused by the fact that people all over the world stopped spending as much money. When they did spend, they looked for cheaper goods from countries other than Britain. This meant that the demand for British **exports** dramatically declined, which led to people losing their jobs, as manufacturers could no longer employ them. As a consequence, by 1932 there were 3 million people out of work in Britain.

The big industrial towns in areas such as South Wales, Clydeside, north-west and north-east England and Northern Ireland were worst affected by unemployment. This was because of long-term problems in the older industries as well as the immediate effects of the Wall Street Crash and Depression. However, the British economy grew in south-east England and the Midlands owing to the growth of new industries manufacturing products such as cars, aeroplanes and electrical goods.

British industry

Much of British industry in the early twentieth century had developed around the coalfields of the North because of its dependence upon steam power. These **old industries** mostly produced **raw materials** or heavy goods, such as ships, textiles (cotton and wool), coal, iron and steel.

The main problem affecting all of the old industries was that they depended on exports. The coal, iron and steel, shipbuilding and textiles industries could only be profitable if they could sell to worldwide markets. From the early 1920s, British industry faced more and more competition from abroad. Often the foreign competitors were much bigger than their British counterparts, so they could produce goods at a price that the small British companies, such as Palmers Shipyard in Jarrow (see page 22), could not compete with.

The situation was made worse by the policies of British governments. They followed a policy of **free trade** in the 1920s. This allowed foreign goods to come into Britain freely. On the other hand,

---

Source A: A map showing areas of heavy unemployment in Britain in the 1930s

Key
■ Areas of heavy unemployment

N

0   150km

Motherwell
Jarrow
Belfast
Maryport
Liverpool
Birmingham
Merthyr
London

British companies that exported goods often had to pay **import duties** to foreign governments.

The worst hit industry of all was shipbuilding. If no one wanted to buy and sell anything, then no new ships were needed to transport goods around. In 1930, British shipbuilders built 1,400,000 tonnes of shipping. In 1933 the figure had fallen to 133,000 tonnes. Unemployment spread from shipbuilding to steelmaking and coal mining. The underlying reasons for the decline in these industries is shown in the table below.

Tasks

1. *Study Source A. Why was there heavy unemployment in these areas in the years after 1931?*

2. *Working in pairs, study the problems facing the four old industries.*

- *Were there any problems common to all four?*
- *What advice would you give to the owners of these industries in the mid-1920s so they could avoid the worst effects of a depression such as that of 1929?*

3. *Does Source B support the view that the old industries were the worst affected? Explain your answer.*

Coal	Textiles
Coal could be produced much more cheaply abroad. In the mid-1920s coal could be produced in the USA for 65p a tonne compared to £1.56 a tonne in Britain. British coal was more expensive because it was more difficult to mine, mines had not invested in up-to-date machinery and the industry was run by coal mine owners who, in most cases, did not want to invest in modernisation.	The market for textiles, such as wool and cotton, declined as man-made fibres, invented in the 1920s, soon became popular. When man-made fibres were mixed with cotton and wool they produced clothes that were more hardwearing and easier to wash. British textile industries also faced increasing competition from Japan and the USA during the 1920s. Both of these countries had developed their own industries during the First World War. Between 1929 and 1939 British textiles industries were reduced in size by 40 per cent.

Iron and steel	Shipbuilding
The iron and steel industry suffered for several reasons. There was far less demand for ships and armaments in the years after the First World War. Competitors such as the USA and Japan regularly undercut British prices and their plants were generally larger, more efficient and modernised than those in Britain.	Shipbuilding declined more rapidly than other industries. There was a fall in world trade in the years after the First World War. This meant less need for ships. International **disarmament** meant a fall in demand for warships. Moreover, foreign countries such as Japan and the USA could produce ships much more cheaply than Britain.

Reasons for the decline of the older industries

Source B: A table showing the percentage of people out of work in the old industries, compared to the national average

Industry	1929	1932	1936
Coal	18	41	25
Cotton	14.5	31	15
Shipbuilding	23	59.5	31
Iron and steel	20	48.5	29.5
National average	10	23	12.5

What measures were brought in by the government to deal with unemployment?

In 1931, a **National Government** was set up to try to reduce unemployment. This was a **coalition** government of the three main parties – Conservative, Liberal and Labour – led by Ramsay MacDonald. There is much debate about the government's actions. Did it do enough to help the depressed areas and the unemployed? There were two main views about the government and the Depression in the 1930s. These are shown in the boxes below.

Source A: Unemployment in Britain in the years 1929–37	
Year	**Approximate number unemployed in millions**
1929	1.4
1930	1.5
1931	2.7
1932	2.8
1933	3.0
1934	2.5
1935	2.4
1936	2.3
1937	1.8

Traditional view

Neville Chamberlain on budget day in 1934. Chamberlain was appointed Chancellor of the Exchequer in the National Government in 1931

The traditional view was that the government should do little to help the economy and the depressed areas. The Depression was part of a natural cycle of boom and slump and would revive itself, especially when world trade increased. The government should concentrate on cutting spending and balancing the budget. This would provide the necessary foundations for recovery. The only intervention would be to place tariffs (taxes) on foreign goods to protect those goods made in Britain.

Spend, Spend, Spend!

John Maynard Keynes

The opposite view to the traditional view was made popular by the British economist John Maynard Keynes. He argued that government spending, especially on public works schemes, would kick-start the economy and provide jobs for the unemployed, whose spending, in turn, would further revive the economy. His ideas were adopted by President F. D. Roosevelt with his **New Deal** policies in the USA and by Adolf Hitler with a programme of public works schemes in Germany, especially the construction of motorways.

The National Government introduced a series of measures to deal with unemployment. Some were short-term to deal with immediate problems with the economy and unemployment whilst others were to provide more long-lasting remedies.

Short-term measures

In 1931, the National Government introduced short-term measures that were designed to restore confidence in Britain abroad and persuade the American banks to lend money to the government.

- Public spending cuts were introduced by cutting the pay of people who worked for the government by 10 per cent. These included teachers, civil servants, the police and the armed forces.
- The National Government also decided to come off the **Gold Standard**. This was where the pound had been valued against British gold reserves which kept the value of the pound high, making exports expensive. Coming off the Gold Standard had the effect of reducing the value of the pound against foreign currencies. British exports became cheaper and imports became more expensive. This helped British exporters and encouraged the British people to buy British.
- To try to tackle the high cost of unemployment benefit, the Means Test was introduced (see pages 14–15) by which the amount of assistance given to the unemployed was based upon their household income.
- Income tax was raised to help to pay for the increased cost of unemployment benefit and the repayment of the loans from the USA.

Longer term measures

In 1932, the National Government tried to prevent an economic crisis ever happening again. It passed the Import Duties Act, which put a 10–20 per cent duty on all imports. They hoped this would encourage British industry to produce and sell more goods. The idea was that if more British goods were bought, more would have to be produced, and so more people would have to be employed to produce them, leading to a fall in unemployment. This benefited new industries such as motor vehicles and electrical goods but had little effect on older industries and areas of higher unemployment. Other countries simply retaliated by putting taxes on goods coming into their country from Britain. This made it more difficult for British export industries.

The government also signed the Ottawa Agreements, which allowed Commonwealth countries to trade with each other on preferential terms. It meant Britain could buy food more cheaply from countries such as Canada, Australia and New Zealand and helped revive trade by providing a market for British exports.

The Exchange Equalisation Account was set up. This kept reserves of gold and foreign currency in Britain. In 1931, the government ran out of foreign currency so could not buy anything from abroad. The Exchange Equalisation Account meant that Britain would not run out of foreign currency again. The exchange control set by the Exchange Equalisation Account lasted until the 1980s.

Source B: Neville Chamberlain, the Chancellor of the Exchequer, defending spending cuts to balance the budget, 1933

*Look around the world today and you see that badly unbalanced budgets are the rule rather than the exception. I find that budget deficits repeated year after year may be accompanied by worsening **recession**. Of all the countries passing through these difficult times the one that has stood the test with the greatest measure of success is the United Kingdom.*

Tasks

1. *Study Source A. What can you learn from Source A about unemployment in Britain in the 1930s? (For guidance on answering this type of question, see page 12.)*

2. *Briefly explain the following measures brought in by the National Government to deal with the problem of unemployment:*
- *Spending cuts*
- *Ottawa Agreements*
- *Exchange Equalisation Account.*

3. *What argument does Chamberlain give in Source B for balancing the budget?*

Helping the older industries

The National Government tried to help the older industries by encouraging smaller companies to join together or amalgamate and adopt a policy of **rationalisation**. **Amalgamation** would, it was hoped, lead to larger companies being more able to compete with their foreign rivals.

Rationalisation meant reducing competition by closing down smaller and less profitable companies. When amalgamation took place, some smaller companies were closed down and the workers sacked. Production was moved to the biggest factories. In many ways this increased rather than reduced the numbers out of work.

The Special Areas Act

As we have seen, the worst hit areas of unemployment were north-east and north-west England, Clydeside, South Wales and Northern Ireland. These became known as the Special Areas.

In 1934, the government passed the Special Areas Act, which offered grants of £2 million to companies that would move to the Special Areas.

Some new industrial estates were created, the first of which was the Team Valley Trading Estate in Gateshead in 1938.

However, unemployment only came down very slowly in those areas. In fact, by 1938, about £8,400,000 had been spent, but only 121 new firms had been set up, creating 14,900 jobs. Small industrial estates could not replace the coal mining or shipbuilding industries. In addition, many companies in the newer industries were reluctant to move to the Special Areas.

> **Source D: From the Third Report of the Commissioners for the Special Areas, 1936**
>
> *There is evidence that the work done and the measures initiated are proving helpful to the Special Areas and that their benefits will in many cases be increasingly felt. Nevertheless, it has to be admitted that there has been no appreciable reduction of the number of those unemployed ... My recommendation is that by means of state-provided inducements a determined attempt should be made to attract industrialists to the Special Areas.*

Source C: A photograph taken by the Special Areas Board of the Team Valley Trading Estate in Gateshead, 1938

How effective were these policies?

The National Government did not believe that government intervention and spending would end the Depression. They were convinced that it was simply a temporary slump and that the economy would revive itself. Although the National Government was prepared to assist companies and areas, it was not prepared to provide large grants or large orders. This meant that the effects of the Depression lasted much longer in Britain than they did in some other countries.

There was also the problem that for many people in Britain the 1930s were a time of increasing prosperity. Those in employment in newer industries, such as motor vehicles and electrical goods, especially in south-east England and the Midlands, often had a relatively good standard of living. It was all too easy for the government to fail to appreciate the impact that the Depression had on the lives of people who lived in the Special Areas.

By the end of the 1930s unemployment had fallen to 1 million. This was only partially due to the policies of the National Government. The main reasons for the fall in unemployment were:

- a revival in world trade from the 1930s, which led to greater demand for British exports
- the policy of **rearmament** which was accelerated in the years after 1935 owing to actions of dictators such as Adolf Hitler in Germany and Benito Mussolini in Italy. The manufacture of military aircraft, ships and munitions provided work for some of the unemployed. It also gave a boost to heavy industries such as coal, iron and steel and shipbuilding.

Source E: A cartoon from the *Daily Express*, 1936

DISTRESSED AREAS

'Work at last'

Tasks

4. *Study Source C and use your own knowledge. What was the purpose of this photograph? Use details from the photograph and your own knowledge to explain your answer. (For guidance on answering this type of question, see page 20.)*

5. *How useful is Source D as evidence of the Special Areas Act being a success?*

6. *What is the message of Source E?*

7. *Make a copy of the scales on the right and write in those measures that helped to reduce unemployment and those that did not.*

8. *'The policies of the National Government helped reduce unemployment.' Do you agree with this statement? Write a brief answer, using the evidence from the scales from task 7, with the main points for and against.*

Measures that reduced unemployment

Measures that did not reduce unemployment

Examination practice

This section provides guidance on how to answer the inference question from Unit 3, which is worth six marks.

Question 1 – inference

Study Source A. What can you learn from Source A about unemployment in Britain in 1932?

> ### Source A: An extract from the *Manchester Evening News*, 15 July 1932
>
> *Two thousand people attended in pouring rain outside the Broadway Theatre, Eccles Cross, today to apply for 35 jobs. Two men had walked from Oldham (a distance of 12 miles [19 kilometres]) and, after being interviewed, were faced with another long walk home in the rain. Applicants were early. Half a dozen waited all night. Some women turned up at a quarter to six. Then the crowd began to gather in earnest. The rain drenched those without overcoats but no one would give up his or her position.*

How to answer

- You are being asked to read between the lines of a source to make inferences about what it tells you about what the question asks – in question 1 this would be unemployment in Britain in 1932.
- In addition, you must support the inferences you make with details from the source.
- Begin your answer with 'Source … suggests that …' In this way you will make a judgement and avoid repeating the contents of the source.
- Look for key words in the source that you can use to make inferences. You could tackle this by highlighting the different points the source makes (as in the example opposite).
- You need to make at least two supported references (there are three examples for Source A opposite).

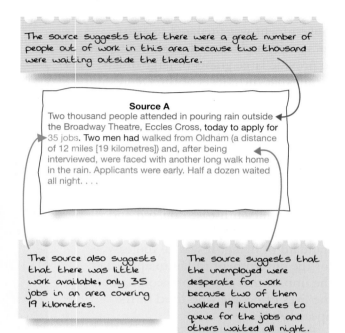

The source suggests that there were a great number of people out of work in this area because two thousand were waiting outside the theatre.

Source A
Two thousand people attended in pouring rain outside the Broadway Theatre, Eccles Cross, today to apply for 35 jobs. Two men had walked from Oldham (a distance of 12 miles [19 kilometres]) and, after being interviewed, were faced with another long walk home in the rain. Applicants were early. Half a dozen waited all night. . . .

The source also suggests that there was little work available, only 35 jobs in an area covering 19 kilometres.

The source suggests that the unemployed were desperate for work because two of them walked 19 kilometres to queue for the jobs and others waited all night.

Now have a go yourself

Try answering question 2 using the steps shown for question 1.

Question 2 – inference

Study Source B. What can you learn from Source B about Britain in the 1930s?

> ### Source B: From *Britain in the Depression*, written in 1994 by J. Stevenson and C. Cook
>
> *It would be silly to suggest that the 1930s were not for many thousands of people a time of great hardship and personal suffering. But beside this picture of the unemployed must be put the other side of the case. There were never less than three-quarters of the population in work during the 1930s. Alongside the pictures of dole queues and hunger marches must also be placed those of another Britain, of new industries, prosperous suburbs and a rising standard of living.*

The experience of the unemployed

Source A: From an article in the *Daily Worker*, 30 January 1933, describing an inquest for Mrs Minnie Weaving, aged 37, of Downham, south-east London. The inquest was told how Mrs Weaving, an unemployed man's wife, literally starved herself to death for her children

George Henry Weaving, the husband, said his wife had not seen a doctor since July, when she had twins. They had seven children living. The coroner asked 'Did she have enough to eat?' Mr Wheating replied 'That is the trouble with us all. I am out of work.'

Dr Arthur Davies, the pathologist, said Mrs Weaving's body was very much wasted and death was due to pneumonia. He added 'I have no doubt that had she had sufficient food this attack would not have proved fatal. It appears that she deliberately starved herself and gave such food as came into the house to the children. She sacrificed her life.'

Task

Study Source A. Suggest a possible headline for this story.

In 1931, the National Government introduced one of the most hated measures of the period, the Means Test, in an attempt to control the amount of help given to the unemployed. This showed little or no understanding of the plight of the families of the long-term unemployed. For those families, especially in the depressed areas, life was very hard. In most cases there was a dramatic fall in living standards, including diet, housing and health. Moreover, long-term unemployment often had negative psychological effects on those out of work.

This chapter answers the following questions:

- Why was the Means Test so unpopular?
- What effects did unemployment have on the standard of living?

Examination skills
In this chapter you will be given guidance on how to answer the source interpretation question, which is worth eight marks.

Why was the Means Test so unpopular?

To try to tackle the high cost of unemployment benefit, the National Government introduced the Means Test in 1931.

After six months on unemployment benefit, people went on to Uncovenanted Benefit, known as the '**dole**'. Before they could receive the dole, people had to have their houses inspected to check all their savings and possessions – that is, go through a means test. The tests were carried out by inspectors from the local Public Assistance Committees (PACs), which had been set up in 1930.

Families could be forced to sell possessions, such as furniture, if they wanted to receive the dole. If a family had any other sources of income, such as a part-time job, or the pension of an elderly relative, deductions were made from the weekly payments. The amount paid was based on the income of the whole family with the maximum payment varying from area to area. The average maximum for a family of two adults and three children was fixed at £1.46, but many were paid less because of earnings from other members of the family. In 1936, the maximum sum was raised to £1.80 but it was still well below the average wage of £3.00.

The Means Test was very unpopular for several reasons:

- Many claimed that it was more about the government trying to save money than helping the unemployed.
- People hated having an inspector go through all of their belongings and then force them to sell some of them.
- People did not like having to make relatives go to live somewhere else if they wanted to get the full amount each week.
- It was humiliating for families to have to reveal their earnings, savings and the value of things they owned.
- If the officials thought that there was enough money in the house they would stop the dole.

- Some local authorities applied the Means Test very harshly. Others, such as those in County Durham, refused to carry it out.
- The Means Test was a great strain on family life, especially if one of the older children, who had a job, was forced to pay more towards family funds.

There were many protests against the Means Test, the most important of which were hunger marches. These were columns of unemployed men who marched across the country trying to bring attention to their plight. The marches began in the autumn of 1931. By the end of 1931 there had been protest marches against the Means Test in more than 30 towns.

However, not all these marches were peaceful. In 1932, there were clashes with the police in Rochdale and Belfast where two demonstrators were killed. The National Unemployed Workers' Movement (NUWM) was set up to try to put pressure on the government. It organised a march on London in October 1932, with marchers attempting to present a petition to Parliament before being stopped by the police.

> ### Source A: From the memoirs of a miner, interviewed in the 1970s, about the Means Test
>
> *My unemployment benefit came to an end in March 1932 when I was disallowed because I had not qualified for the necessary contributory period of thirty weeks. After this I was given a food ticket for £1.15, which continued until January 1933, when it was stopped because of the Means Test. So now we have to depend on the boys and they have to keep all six of us including my wife and the two children who are still going to school.*

Source C: From *The Road to Wigan Pier*, written by George Orwell in 1937

The Means Test breaks up families. An old age pensioner would usually live with one of his children. Under the Means Test, he counts as a 'lodger' and his children's dole will be cut.

Source D: An unemployed man describes the effects of the Means Test on his life

My wife obtained a job as a house-to-house saleswoman, and was able to earn a few shillings to supplement our dole income. This strained our relationship. It was a burden on her and constant bickerings over money matters, usually culminating in threats to leave from both of us. The final blow came when the Means Test was put into operation. Eventually, after the most heartbreaking period of my life, both my wife and son, who had just begun to earn a few shillings, told me to get out, as I was living on them and taking the food they needed.

Tasks

1. *Study Sources A, C and D. How far do these sources agree about the effects of the Means Test? Explain your answer, using the sources. (For guidance on answering this type of question, see pages 45–46.)*

2. *How useful are Sources B and D as evidence of the Means Test? Explain your answer, using Sources B and D and your own knowledge. (For guidance on answering this type of question, see pages 68–70.)*

3. *Work in pairs. Imagine you had to advertise the protest march against the Means Test shown in Source B. Produce a poster criticising the Means Test and encouraging people to take part in the march.*

What effects did unemployment have on the standard of living?

In the areas of Britain where the old industries had grown up, such as Cumbria, South Wales and Central Scotland, unemployment soon became very high, sometimes over 50 per cent, and lasted a long time. This long-term unemployment often led to a fall in the standard of living and health of the families of those out of work.

Poverty and diet

For the poor, or for those without jobs, the 1930s was a time of hardship and suffering.

Seebohm Rowntree, a social researcher and son of the chocolate manufacturer Joseph Rowntree, carried out a survey of York at the beginning of the twentieth century and found that 30 per cent of people in York lived below the **poverty line**. In 1936, Rowntree completed a second survey and found this percentage had remained the same. Moreover, his findings revealed that 72.6 per cent of unemployed workers lived below the poverty line.

More evidence of hardship is shown in a survey of Stockton-on-Tees in the early 1930s. This compared the average weekly income of a family in which the wage earner was out of work with that of a family in which he was in work. The average weekly income of an unemployed family was £1.46. For an employed family the average income was £2.57.

Families of the unemployed had less to spend and had to make whatever savings they could. One way was to buy cheaper food but cheaper food could lead to malnutrition. The same survey in Stockton-on-Tees showed that a poor family was likely to spend only 3 shillings (15p) a head on food per week, while a richer family would spend at least 6 shillings (30p).

> **Source A:** From an interview in 1935 with the wife of an unemployed shipyard worker
>
> *If only he had work. Just imagine what it would be like. On the whole my husband has worked about one year out of twelve and a half. His face was lovely when I married him, but now he's skin and bones. When we married he had a good job. He was earning £8 to £10 a week. He's a left-handed ship's riveter, a craft which should be earning him a lot of money. He fell out of work about four months after I was married so I've hardly known what a week's wages was.*

> **Source B:** A table showing the weekly spending of the family of an unemployed textile worker in Lancashire in 1931. Their weekly dole payment was £1.59

Item	Weekly spending
Rent	43p
Coal	17½p
Gas	12½p
Union and insurance subscription	16p
Savings club	5p
Meat	10p
Milk	12½p
Bread	23½p
Margarine	10p
Jam	4p
Clog-irons	2½p
Total	£1.56½

Source C: From *The Road to Wigan Pier*, written by George Orwell in 1937

It will be seen that the income of a family on the dole normally averages around £1.50 a week. One can write at least a quarter of this off as rent. A man and wife on £1.15 a week are not far from the starvation line but they can make a home of sorts. They are vastly better off than the single man on 75p. He lives in a common lodging house, more often a furnished room, for which he usually pays 30p a week. So he spends his days in the public library or any other place where he can keep warm.

In 1936, John Boyd Orr published the results of a survey into the diets and health of the British people. He concluded that 4.5 million people had a diet that was completely inadequate in all respects. A further 5 million people suffered from some forms of deficiency. Overall he believed that one tenth of the population was seriously under-nourished. This percentage included one fifth of all children.

Families of the unemployed ate much bread, margarine, potato, sugar and tea but little meat, fresh fruit and vegetables and milk. The diets of wives and mothers were most inadequate as they sacrificed their own needs for those of their husbands and children.

Source D: From a television interview with Frank Cousins, a trade union leader, in 1966

I happened to be in a transport café on the Great North Road, when a young couple came in with a child in a nearly broken-down pram. They were walking from South Shields (near Newcastle) to London because the man understood he could get a job. They sat down and fed the baby with water. They lifted the baby's dress up. She was wearing a newspaper nappy. They took it off and sort of wiped the baby's bottom with the nappy they'd taken off and then picked up another newspaper and put that on for another nappy. I immediately thought someone ought to do something about this situation.

Tasks

1. Study Source A. What can you learn from Source A about the effects of unemployment? (Remember how to answer this type of question? For guidance, see page 12.)

2. Study Sources B, C and D. How far do these sources agree about the dole providing enough income to live on? Explain your answer, using the sources. (For guidance on answering this type of question, see pages 45–46.)

3. How useful are Sources C and D as evidence of the effects of unemployment? Explain your answer, using Sources C and D and your own knowledge. (For guidance on answering this type of question, see pages 68–70.)

Women

Women often suffered worst of all during the Depression. They were generally the first to be laid off, especially in the cotton industry, which had employed large numbers of women. In contrast, the number of women in domestic service went up in the 1930s, as women looked for any chance of finding work.

In addition, **National Insurance** usually only covered the worker, which would normally be the man. That meant that women and children were often not covered for medical treatment. They would have to pay for visits to the doctor and for any medicine. Furthermore, many women sacrificed themselves to feed their children or pay for their medical treatment rather than their own.

Government statistics showed that from 1931 to 1935 the **death rate** for women aged 15 to 35 was more than twice as high in some areas of high unemployment as it was in other areas.

Health and housing

One of the consequences of poverty and poor diet was the higher **infant mortality rate** and poorer health of children in depressed areas. For example, in the South-East in 1935, the infant death rate was 42 per 1000 live births. In Northumberland and Durham it was 76. As well as the difference in the death rate in different regions there was also a difference between rich and poor. For example, in the 1930s, for every three children from richer families who died young, there were eight children from poorer families.

Local medical officers of health frequently reported on the poor health of districts in the depressed areas. In 1933, an investigation in Newcastle revealed that one in three schoolchildren were physically unfit because of poor health. Comparisons with children from richer families showed that the poor were ten times more likely to catch bronchitis, eight times more likely to catch pneumonia and five times more likely to suffer from rickets.

Overcrowded living conditions contributed to poor health. In 1935 a survey concluded that 12 per cent of the people of Britain lived at least two to a room. In some parts of central London there were three to four families living in each house and many of these families lived in one room.

> **Source F:** From a radio discussion about housing, broadcast in 1933. One of the speakers got out a newspaper parcel while he was speaking and pulled from it a large, dead rat
>
> *I live in a house in which there are six families in seven rooms, 31 people in all. My family live in a damp basement. There are seven of us, all sleeping in one room. It is in need of such repair that we cannot leave the babies alone because of the rats. We hear them scratching at night. I brought one along with me. We caught it in the gas oven this afternoon.*

Source E: A photograph of a street in Wigan in 1939

The psychological effects

One common consequence of unemployment was mental suffering. Investigators found a general trend. The first week or so of unemployment was treated as a holiday. The unemployed got up early, put on their best clothes and went down to the local labour exchange to seek work.

After a few weeks, confidence began to go, expectations fell and the unemployed took less interest in personal appearance. Many, used to being the breadwinner, felt guilty and lost all self-respect and self-esteem.

> **Source G: From *Love on the Dole*, a novel written by Walter Greenwood in the 1930s**
>
> *It got to you slowly like a malignant disease. You fell into the habit of slouching, of putting your hands in your pockets and keeping them there. Of glancing at people secretly, ashamed of your secret. You prayed for the winter evenings and the kindly darkness. Pants with the backside patched and re-patched; patches on knees, on elbows. Jesus! All bloody patches.*

Tasks

4. *Working in pairs, imagine you are campaigning for better conditions for the unemployed. Devise captions you would use for Sources E and H.*

5. *Study Source G. Pick out key words or phrases used by Greenwood to put across his message.*

6. *How reliable are Sources F and G as evidence of the impact of the Depression on the lives of the unemployed? Explain your answer, using Sources F and G and your own knowledge. (For guidance on answering this type of question, see page 87.)*

7. *Create a mind map showing the effects of unemployment on the families of the unemployed. In your mind map, prioritise the effects clockwise, beginning with the most serious to the least serious.*

8. *Study Sources A–H on pages 16–19. 'The worst effect of the Depression was on the income of the families of the unemployed.' How far do Sources A–H support this statement? Use details from the sources and your own knowledge to explain your answer. (For guidance on answering this type of question, see pages 96–98.)*

Source H: A photograph taken in 1936. It shows men reading newspapers in an unemployment club

Examination practice

This section provides guidance on how to answer the source interpretation question from Unit 3, which is worth eight marks.

Question 1 – source interpretation

Study Source A and use your own knowledge. What was the purpose of this poster? Use details from the poster and your own knowledge to explain your answer.

How to answer

You are being asked to explain why the source was produced. In order to do this you need to:

- examine carefully the details of the source and use these to back up your answer
- make inferences from the source. What is it suggesting? What is its tone or attitude? What is the overall message? Use details from the source to back up your answer.

Purpose
To highlight the plight of the unemployed in order to encourage more support for the hunger march and to prompt the government into making improvements and changes.

Inference
Unemployed families are suffering from a poor diet.

Details
This shows one of key grievances of the marchers.

Inference
Current relief payments are inadequate.

Overall message
The Means Test is unfair and they need more help from the government.

- explain the purpose of the source. This is the most important skill which, if carried out successfully, will lead to higher level marks. In other words, what is the source trying to make you think? Is it trying to get you to support or oppose a person or event? Use details from the source to back up your answer.
- support your answer on the purpose of the source with your own contextual knowledge – in other words, your knowledge of what was going on at that time that involves the person or event. In this case you can explain about some or all of the following: the Means Test; underfed families; hunger marches.

To plan an answer to this question, you could annotate the source as shown in the example below. Part of an answer showing how to support the inferences from the source with contextual knowledge is also given below.

> **Source A: A reconstruction of part of a poster by the Clydeside Communist Party, June 1934**
>
> **THE SCOTTISH HUNGER MARCH**
> TO THE WORKERS OF SCOTLAND!
> THE DEMANDS
>
> As against the government's policy we are demanding that the workers and their dependants who are victims of unemployment, be properly fed. With this aim in view we ask that the Secretary of State for Scotland meet the Marchers' deputation on Monday 12 June to discuss the following demands:
>
> (1) Abolition of the Means Test.
> (2) That children of the unemployed be granted 1/6d. [8p] per week extra and that adult unemployed and adult dependants be granted 3/6d. [17p] per week extra.
> (3) That rents be reduced by 25%.
> (4) That relief work be provided for the unemployed.

Source A suggests that the dole is totally inadequate for families on Clydeside and is leading to a poor diet. The overall message of the poster is that the Means Test is unfair and the dole is inadequate for unemployed families. The purpose of the poster is to encourage opposition to the Means Test and support for those groups, such as the Clydeside Communist Party, who wanted the measure removed as well as their hunger march. Hunger marches were a popular method of protest against the Means Test in the mid-1930s.

The Jarrow Crusade

Source A: **A photograph of a life-size statue entitled** *The Spirit of Jarrow*, **created in 2001 to commemorate the 65th anniversary of the Jarrow Crusade**

Task

What does Source A suggest about the importance of the Jarrow March?

As we have seen, hunger marches were one reaction to long-term unemployment. The purpose of hunger marches was to publicise the conditions of the unemployed and to try to bring about government intervention. The most famous hunger march took place from Jarrow to London in 1936 and became known as the Jarrow Crusade. It captured the imagination of many people at the time. However, it made little difference to the situation in Jarrow itself.

This chapter answers the following questions:

- Why was the Jarrow March organised?
- What happened during the Jarrow March?
- What did the Jarrow March achieve?

Examination skills

In this chapter you will be given the opportunity to answer some of the different question types from Unit 3.

Why was the Jarrow March organised?

The worst affected town of all during the Depression was Jarrow, near Newcastle. This was because most people in the town depended upon one shipyard for their livelihood. The vast majority of the population were either employed by or dependent on one firm, Palmers Shipyard.

The shipyard began to decline after the First World War. There were fewer warships being built and after 1929 fewer and fewer cargo ships. In the early 1930s, orders dried up completely. Unemployment rose from 3245 in 1929 to 7178 in 1933. Palmers also suffered from another problem. By the 1930s the yard was really too small for the type of ship that was being built. The Queen Elizabeth and Queen Mary, which were launched in the 1930s, were over 80,000 tonnes. Palmers just could not match that.

The end came in 1934. A group of shipyard owners set up National Shipbuilders' Security Ltd. They decided to buy up smaller yards and then scrap them. Palmers was one of the first to go. In 1934, it was bought up and the yard was closed. It was announced that no ships would be built there for 40 years. This had a terrible effect on Jarrow. Unemployment reached 80 per cent at one point.

Normal life almost ceased to exist as families tried to find any way that they could to survive. The death rates and infant mortality rates in Jarrow were monitored by the Jarrow Public Health Committee and published. The figures for Jarrow were very high, which shows that malnutrition and poor health were widespread in the town. The local authorities were aware of the problems being caused, but were able to do little about them. Families were totally dependent upon support from the local community or the government. The problem was that in Jarrow there were thousands of families like this. And the local community simply could not cope with the situation.

Tasks

1. Study Source A. Who does Ellen Wilkinson blame for the closure of Palmers?

2. What does Source B suggest about Jarrow in the 1930s?

Source A: From *The Town that was Murdered*, written in 1938 by Ellen Wilkinson, the Labour MP for Jarrow

In 1930, National Shipbuilders' Security Ltd was set up. This company bought up and scrapped one-third of the British shipbuilding industry in an alleged attempt to save yards from the economic collapse. NSS were able by the financial weakness of Palmers to buy it up at scrap prices. Holders of the ordinary shares, such as the workmen, who in better days had invested their savings, were left with worthless paper. Protests were made, but nothing effective could be done unless the government was prepared to act.

Source B: A table showing death rates and infant mortality rates 1919–36

Death rates per 1000 of population			
	1919	1931	1936
Jarrow	20	15	15
National average	13	10	9
Infant mortality – deaths (0–1 year) per 1000 of population			
	1919	1931	1936
Jarrow	151	159	114
National average	58	62	57

Source C: From *English Journey* by J. B. Priestley, 1934, an account of the author's travels through England. Here Priestley describes his visit to Jarrow in 1933

I have seen nothing like it since the First World War. There is no escape anywhere from the prevailing misery. One out of every two shops is closed. Wherever we went there were men hanging about, not scores of them but hundreds and thousands of them. The men wore the drawn masks of prisoners of war.

The people of Jarrow sent a number of deputations to the Board of Trade in London. They got nowhere. In 1936, the last deputation met the President of the Board of Trade, a cabinet minister who told them to go back to Jarrow and work out their own salvation. In 1936, Jarrow made one last effort. A march was organised by the people of the town from Jarrow to London. The object was to attract attention to the plight of the town by taking a petition all the way to parliament.

However, the government was very suspicious of hunger marchers, such as those from Jarrow. This was because one of the leaders of previous hunger marches, Will Hannington, was a **communist**, which alarmed the authorities, and the marches had often led to clashes with the police. Stanley Baldwin, the Prime Minister, was especially unsympathetic towards hunger marches. Moreover, the Trades Union Congress (TUC) and Labour Party did not support these marches, believing they only brought bad publicity for the labour movement and the plight of the unemployed. Moreover, the Jarrow Crusade was one of the few hunger marches of the 1930s not run by the National Unemployed Workers' Movement (NUWM). Indeed the NUWM actually opposed the march for two reasons:

- The Jarrow marchers refused to co-operate with a much larger march organised by the NUWM in which several groups were to converge on London at the same time.
- The NUWM objected to the non-political nature of the Jarrow March. The Jarrow marchers did not favour any of the political parties with both Labour and Conservative party officials helping with its organisation.

Source D: David Riley, the organiser of the Jarrow March, speaking in 1936

I think we should get down to London with a couple of bombs in our pockets. These people do not realise that there are people living in Jarrow today in conditions in which a respectable farmer would not keep pigs. We must do something outrageous which will make the country sit up.

Source E: Joe Symonds, speaking on the radio in 1979. He was one of the marchers

We decided, why not march to London? We can show them that with all our trouble we still have a bit of spirit left.

Source F: From an account written by the mayor of Jarrow in 1936

A campaign was started by the Labour Party to send a petition. Then it was decided to march with the petition. I opposed the decision. There were hunger marches going on all over and I didn't want to embarrass and put down the men. I eventually had to agree, and I marched to Darlington with some of the men. I managed to get time off from Spiller's in Newcastle. Communists wanted to join us on the march, but we wouldn't let them.

Tasks

3. *Using the evidence on these two pages and Source A on page 21, put together a poster advertising the Jarrow March.*

4. *What is the message of Source C? How does Priestley put across this message?*

5. *Study Sources D, E and F. How far do these sources agree about the reasons for the Jarrow March? Explain your answer, using the sources. (For guidance on answering this type of question, see pages 45–46.)*

What happened during the Jarrow March?

The Jarrow March was carefully planned and prepared and the final route decided. The marchers covered over 450 kilometres in 22 stages as shown in the map below.

Eventually 200 men marched from Jarrow to London, led by the mayor, the MP Ellen Wilkinson and town councillors. They marched in step in their best clothes so that they would have the greatest possible impact on the people that they passed. The men were turned out as smartly as possible and were clean-shaven.

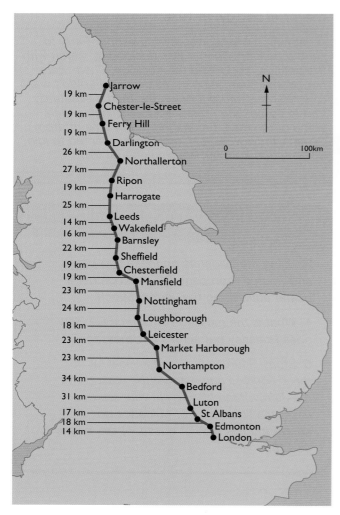

The route taken by the marchers on the Jarrow Crusade

Source A: Ritchie Calder, a journalist who covered the march

In one family there were four volunteers from whom only one could go. And the brothers gave the trousers and jacket and the father gave the boots and the uncle gave the raincoat … the family marched with one man.

Source B: From a memo by the Special Branch of the Metropolitan Police, 1936

The promoters of the march from Jarrow to London have now made definite arrangements for 200 marchers to take the road on the 5th October. The plans are being carried out by Miss Ellen Wilkinson MP, a former communist.

Tasks

1. *Study Source A. What can you learn from Source A about the preparations for the march? (Remember how to answer this type of question? For guidance, see page 12.)*

2. *Study Source B. Why do you think the Special Branch was reporting on the preparations for the march?*

Source C: Sam Rowan being interviewed in 1982. He worked for the Jarrow council in 1936 and was sent to prepare the way for the marchers

Our first stop was Chester-le-Street and we stopped in the field and our cooks made tea and dished out corned beef sandwiches. And I can assure you the men were looking forward to it. But the next stop we had at Ferry Hill, and there the miners went to town. We had a dozen chefs in white hats and everything.

Source D: A photograph of the Jarrow marchers, with Ellen Wilkinson at the front

As the marchers made their way south, they were completely surprised by the reception that they received. Everywhere they went they received great support and sympathy. They were put up in church halls and given free meals and their shoes were repaired free of charge. The Bishop of Ripon spoke out in their support and newspapers published accounts of their progress. But when they arrived in London, there was little support or sympathy from members of the government.

Source E: A photograph of the Jarrow marchers stopping for a meal near Bedford

Tasks

3. *Working in pairs, study the two photographs of the march – Sources D and E. Put together headlines to accompany the photos that could have been made by newspapers supporting the march.*

4. *Study Source D and use your own knowledge. What was the purpose of this photograph? Use details from the photograph and your own knowledge to explain your answer. (Remember how to answer this type of question? For guidance, see page 20.)*

5. *Study Sources C and F. How far do these sources agree about the Jarrow March?*

6. *How useful are Sources E and F as evidence of the Jarrow March? (For guidance on answering this type of question, see pages 68–70.)*

Source F: Ellen Wilkinson, writing in the *North Eastern Gazette*, after the march

It was a great help, the action of the boot repairers of the Leicester Co-operative Society who worked till midnight without pay mending the boots that so badly needed repair by then. The hospital students provided by the Socialist Medical Association literally kept the men on their feet. Free cinema tickets from cinema managers at every town we stayed in. Kindness all the way. So many passing motorists raised their hats as we passed that we began to feel like celebrities.

What did the Jarrow March achieve?

There is much debate over the achievements of the Jarrow March. On the one hand, it has been seen as providing much needed publicity for the plight of the unemployed in general and Jarrow in particular. On the other hand, some have argued that little was actually achieved.

Its achievements

The Jarrow petition was presented to the House of Commons. The petition mentioned the closure of the shipyard and the high number of unemployed. It asked the government to provide work for the town 'without delay'.

In addition the marchers were given much support from the public during the actual march. The march improved the public image of hunger marches, some of which had previously led to clashes with the police. Indeed the police praised the marchers for being well organised and disciplined. The men returned to Jarrow as heroes.

Its limitations

The march and the petition did little or nothing to stir the government into action. Stanley Baldwin refused to make any comment on being presented with the petition. His response was predictable. He had the reputation of not giving in to external pressure. In 1926, he had forced the **General Strike** to come to an end and he did the same in 1936 by ignoring the Jarrow marchers' petition.

> **Source A:** Guy Waller, a journalist, writing in 1936
>
> *The march produced no immediate startling upsurge in employment to the town. It took the war to do that.*

> **Source B:** From an article in the *Guardian* newspaper in 2003 about the Jarrow March
>
> *When they arrived, Ellen Wilkinson handed in a petition of nearly 12,000 Jarrow signatures at the Palace of Westminster. Despite widespread public sympathy for the marchers and the plight of the people of Tyneside, Baldwin refused to see them or their representatives. Their demonstration at Hyde Park Corner was sparsely attended.*

> **Source C:** From a letter from the Bishop of Durham to *The Times*, October 1936
>
> *The policy of the marches is, in my view, a revolutionary policy. It involves substituting organised mob rule for the proper constitutional way of doing things.*

> **Source D:** From the memories of the Jarrow March by Kathleen Haigh who was interviewed for Radio Newcastle
>
> *My uncle, Jimmy McCauley, was the second last of the marchers to die. He said he wore out many pairs of shoes on the march and that all of the marchers looked forward to being fed by the people in whichever town they arrived! In retrospect, he believed that the march was in vain because nothing happened afterwards to bring jobs to the town. The legacy which does remain is that Jarrow has found its place in history thanks to their brave efforts.*

Source F: **From a history of Britain between the wars**

The Jarrow marchers wanted to obtain jobs to support their families and also find recognition and respect for themselves and other workers throughout the country. The marchers had no food or money, but they received great support from the public. Wherever the marchers stopped overnight, local people would give them shelter and food, and even provide them with boots to enable them to continue. The route was 280 miles [451 kilometres] and took 22 days. They achieved much needed publicity for the plight of the unemployed in general and the town of Jarrow in particular.

Tasks

1. *Study Sources B, D and F. Do Sources B and D support the evidence of Source F about the Jarrow Crusade? Explain your answer, using the sources. (For guidance on answering this type of question, see pages 45–46.)*

2. *Study Source C. What can you learn from Source C about the Jarrow Crusade? (Remember how to answer this type of question? For guidance, see page 12.)*

3. *How useful are Sources A and E as evidence of the Jarrow Crusade? Explain your answer, using Sources A and E and your own knowledge. (For guidance on answering this type of question, see pages 68–70.)*

Key Topic 2: Britain alone

Source A: **A photograph of St Paul's Cathedral, London, during the Blitz, December 1941. The cathedral was left intact, despite the damage all around**

Task

Look at Source A. What message is the photographer trying to put across?

The defeat of France in June 1940 meant that for a year Britain alone faced the threat from Nazi Germany until the German invasion of the Soviet Union in June 1941. The British survived for several reasons, most especially the leadership of Winston Churchill, victory in the Battle of Britain and the failure of the German **Blitz** of British cities and towns.

Each chapter explains a key issue and examines important lines of enquiry as outlined below.

Chapter 4: The British Expeditionary Force (BEF), Dunkirk and Churchill (pages 29–38)
- What was the Phoney War?
- Why did the BEF retreat to Dunkirk in 1940?
- What happened at Dunkirk in May–June 1940?
- How was Britain able to survive Dunkirk?

Chapter 5: The Battle of Britain (pages 39–46)
- What happened during the Battle of Britain?
- Why was the RAF successful?
- What was the importance of the Battle of Britain?

Chapter 6: The Blitz (pages 47–57)
- What were the effects of the Blitz of 1940–41?
- What measures were taken to deal with the Blitz?
- What were the key features of evacuation?
- What were the effects of the second Blitz, 1944–45?

The British Expeditionary Force (BEF), Dunkirk and Churchill

4

Task

Study Source A. What can you learn from Source A about the retreat of the British Expeditionary Force (BEF) to Dunkirk in 1940? (Remember how to answer this type of question? For guidance, see page 12.)

Source A: From *1940: Myth and Reality*, Clive Ponting, 1990

*The morale, cohesion and discipline of the **British Expeditionary Force** (BEF) was poor as it moved towards Dunkirk. There was a lack of food and many soldiers looted what they required from the Belgians. When the first British troops arrived at Dunkirk, discipline nearly broke down altogether. On 29 May, French troops were manhandled off British ships and soldiers from the two armies came close to shooting each other. For the first two days of the evacuation, order had to be kept by armed naval personnel. Even then soldiers were rushing the boats in their anxiety to get away. Large numbers of officers ran away and deserted their troops so as to get on to the earliest boat.*

Britain declared war on Germany on 3 September 1939 following the invasion of Poland. There was very little fighting for the next few months and this period of the war became known initially as the 'Bore War' and then the 'Phoney War'. It was only in April 1940 that fighting really began when Germany invaded Denmark and Norway. On 10 May, the day Churchill became Britain's Prime Minister, Hitler ordered the invasion of the Low Countries but by the end of the month British forces had been pushed back to Dunkirk, from where they were able to retreat across the Channel. On 21 June, the French surrendered, leaving Britain to face Germany on its own.

This chapter answers the following questions:

- What was the Phoney War?
- Why did the BEF retreat to Dunkirk in 1940?
- What happened at Dunkirk in May–June 1940?
- How was Britain able to survive Dunkirk?

Examination skills

In this chapter you will be given guidance on how to answer the cross-referencing question, which is worth ten marks.

What was the Phoney War?

Britain declared war on Germany on 3 September 1939 following the invasion of Poland. At first, there was little fighting on the **Western Front**. The British Expeditionary Force (BEF), under the command of Lord Gort, was sent over to France and Belgium on a gradual basis. Initially, it had four infantry divisions and 50 light tanks. The British and French built up their forces and the French continued to anticipate a frontal assault on the Franco–German border where the French had built a series of extremely well-armed forts, minefields and trenches (this was the Maginot Line).

By May 1940, the BEF had increased in size and had six more divisions giving a total of almost 400,000 men. The period of military inactivity from September 1939 to April 1940 is known as the 'Phoney War'.

The 'Phoney War' came to an end on 9 April 1940, when Hitler invaded Denmark and Norway. By capturing these two countries he would safeguard his supply of iron ore and ensure that he could sustain his military campaigns. Furthermore, if Norway were captured, the entrance to the Baltic Sea would be secured and, in addition, Germany would have North Sea bases from which to attack Britain. Controlling the Norwegian ports would also make it more difficult for the British navy to create an effective blockade of Germany.

Source A: **A photograph of reinforcements for the British Expeditionary Force on board a troop transport ship to cross the Channel to France in May 1940**

The British campaign in Norway

Britain decided to send troops to support Norway but the land campaign was an utter failure. Britain's soldiers were inadequately prepared and equipped and insufficient air support was provided. By early June 1940, all British troops were withdrawn. British and Norwegian losses were about 3000. During the struggle for Norway, the German navy lost several destroyers and cruisers. This meant that their surface fleet was no longer able to confront the British navy and this had repercussions for Hitler at the end of May 1940, when British forces retreated across the Channel (see page 34). Moreover, the losses meant that Hitler did not have enough ships to carry out his invasion of Britain.

The impact of the Norwegian campaign on Britain

Defeat in Norway brought renewed pressure on Britain's Prime Minister, Neville Chamberlain. Despite the fact that the campaign had been the idea of Winston Churchill, Chamberlain had to shoulder the burden of blame for its abject failure. In the parliamentary debate that followed the withdrawal from Norway, many of Chamberlain's Conservative Party colleagues attacked him and demanded his resignation. Chamberlain won the vote following the debate, but he knew that he no longer had the support and confidence of the Conservative Party. Having lost his party's support, he resigned on 10 May 1940 just as Hitler launched his *Blitzkrieg* on Holland and Belgium. (Blitzkrieg is German for 'Lightning War'. It involved the use of aeroplanes, tanks and motorised troops to achieve speed and surprise.) Britain faced two huge issues – the war had erupted in the West and its Prime Minister had resigned.

Tasks

1. *What is meant by the terms BEF, Maginot Line and Phoney War?*

2. *What does Source A tell you about the BEF in May 1940?*

3. *What does Source B suggest about British attitudes towards the German invasion of Norway?*

4. *Explain why the Norwegian campaign was important for Britain.*

Source B: **A cartoon from the *Daily Sketch*, April 1940, commenting on the German invasion of Norway. The *Daily Sketch* was a British newspaper**

'NECESSITY KNOWS NO LAW' - - - By CLIVE UPTTON

The role of Winston Churchill

On 10 May 1940, Winston Churchill was appointed Prime Minister of Britain. Churchill detested Hitler and **Nazism** and had spoken out against Germany throughout the 1930s. He knew that he had to rally the British people and his first speech as Prime Minister to the House of Commons set the tone for what he expected. Churchill provided the strong leadership needed during this difficult period. He kept up the morale of the British people and made them believe in ultimate victory with speeches and tours of the country. His speeches were so powerful that it was said that he 'mobilised the English language' as part of the war effort. There was no talk of surrender and he rejected any idea of peace. For him the defeat of Nazism was all that mattered.

Biography Winston Churchill 1874–1965

1874 Born at Blenheim Palace
1900 Elected Conservative MP
1904 Joined the Liberal Party
1910 Home Secretary
1911–1915 First Lord of the Admiralty
1917 Minister of Munitions
1918–1921 Secretary of State for War and Air
1921–22 Colonial Secretary
1922 Re-joined the Conservative Party
1924–29 Chancellor of the Exchequer
1929–39 Out of office
1939 First Lord of the Admiralty
1940–45 Prime Minister and Minister of Defence

Source C: US cartoon of June 1940 depicting Churchill as a British bulldog

HOLDING THE LINE !

Source D: Part of Winston Churchill's speech to the House of Commons, 13 May 1940

I would say to the House, as I said to those who have joined this government: 'I have nothing to offer but blood, toil, tears and sweat.'

We have before us many, many long months of struggle and of suffering. You ask, what is our policy? It is to wage war, by sea, land and air, with all our might and with all the strength that God can give us; to wage war against a monstrous tyranny, never surpassed in the dark, lamentable catalogue of human crime. That is our policy.

You ask, what is our aim? I can answer in one word: It is victory, victory at all costs, victory in spite of all terror, victory, however long and hard the road may be; for without victory, there is no survival. At this time I feel entitled to claim the aid of all, and I say, 'Come then, let us go forward together with our united strength.'

Tasks

5. Explain what the phrase 'mobilised the English language' means.

6. What message is the cartoonist trying to put across in Source C?

7. *Study Source D. What can you learn from Source D about Winston Churchill as a leader of people?*
(Remember how to answer this type of question? For guidance, see page 12.)

Why did the BEF retreat to Dunkirk in 1940?

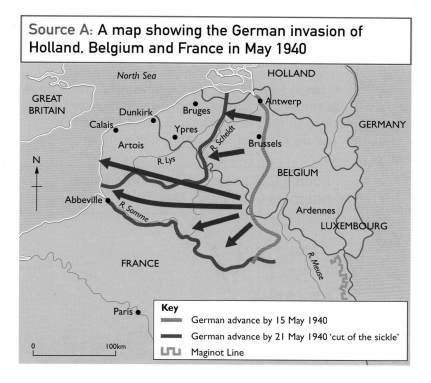

Source A: A map showing the German invasion of Holland, Belgium and France in May 1940

Key
- German advance by 15 May 1940
- German advance by 21 May 1940 'cut of the sickle'
- Maginot Line

The German attack on Belgium and Holland on 10 May 1940 caught the BEF and French forces unawares. The expected German attack had been from across the border where the Maginot Line had been constructed. There was an expectation that these fortifications would serve as a protector and shield. However, Hitler ordered the attack into France to go through Belgium and then the Ardennes. This was a further shock because the French and British had assumed that the Ardennes was unsuitable for tank warfare because it was a hilly and wooded area. Moreover, the River Meuse was another natural barrier to the *Blitzkrieg* attack.

However, the defeat of the French in just a few weeks was most astonishing. The German tank divisions went through the Ardennes in two days and crossed the River Meuse without any major setbacks. The French troops here were swept aside. In the northern part of the *Blitzkrieg*, it took five days to defeat Holland. After a huge bombing raid on Rotterdam, which killed about 1000 people,

the Dutch surrendered. Thirteen days after the Dutch surrender, Belgium surrendered. *Blitzkrieg* had worked again. As the German army continued to move into France, part of it moved north to encircle the BEF and part moved south-west towards Paris.

During the movement of German troops into Belgium, British and French forces moved to its border to support their ally. However, the German forces quickly moved across the River Meuse, outflanked the British and French and moved to the coast beyond Abbeville. By 20 May, huge numbers of the BEF and French army found themselves cut off from the rest of their forces. More importantly, they were cut off from their supply bases. The Germans called this phase of their *Blitzkrieg* attack 'the cut of the sickle' (see map).

On 21 May, the BEF, led by Lord Gort, attempted to break out of the area of land created by the 'cut of the sickle', but failed. Lord Gort then decided that British forces should retreat to Dunkirk and try to retreat across the Channel with as many of his soldiers as possible. It was at this time that the British were most fortunate. On 20 May, Hitler gave the order to halt his *Panzerkampfwagen* (tanks) in order to allow the *Luftwaffe* (German air force) to complete the destruction of the British and French forces.

Tasks

1. *What does Source A tell you about the German attack on Western Europe?*

2. *Create a mind map showing the reasons why the BEF was forced to retreat to Dunkirk.*

What happened at Dunkirk in May–June 1940?

Hitler's decision to halt his tanks turned out to be an error. It allowed the British a breathing space and a time to re-group. As defensive perimeters were developed, the Royal Navy and a host of vessels ranging from yachts to pleasure boats and paddle steamers crossed the Channel to rescue the stranded troops and their equipment. Initially, there was chaos in Dunkirk, but eventually some semblance of order and discipline was established.

The evacuation lasted nine days and was further helped by the British soldiers who were surrounded at Calais. Again, the Germans made an error and decided to capture Calais rather than move on to Dunkirk. It has been estimated that the action at Calais gave the British three extra days to evacuate their forces at Dunkirk.

The evacuation, codenamed Operation Dynamo, began on 27 May when almost 8000 troops were picked up. The last day was 4 June when more than 26,000 landed back in Britain. The small boats, known as 'Little ships', were able to pick up men from the beaches. They ferried them to larger vessels in the Channel or took them to the nearest English port. Some protection was given to the troops on the beaches by the RAF and the German *Luftwaffe* did sustain losses.

Source A: From a report in a British newspaper, the *Daily Mail*, 1 June 1940

An artilleryman told me that with thousands of others he had spent two days among the sand dunes with little food and no shelter from the German dive-bombers. Yet men still joked, played cards and even started a football game to keep their spirits up. A sailor told me that the vessel he was on had been sunk off the Belgian coast. No sooner had he and all his comrades landed in England than they volunteered to go back to France at once.

Source B: From a book about the Dunkirk evacuation, published in 1975

There were accounts of a hotel cellar in Dunkirk with British and French troops singing, weeping and very drunk. There were groups of men deserted by their officers. A corporal kept order in his boat, filled with troops crazy with fear, by threatening to shoot the first one who disobeyed him.

Source C: A photograph of 'Little ships' returning to England, May 1940

Tasks

1. *Study Source A. What can you learn from Source A about the evacuation from Dunkirk in 1940? (Remember how to answer this type of question? For guidance, see page 12.)*

2. *How useful are Sources A and B as evidence of the evacuation from Dunkirk? Explain your answer, using sources A and B and your own knowledge. (For guidance on answering this type of question, see pages 68–70.)*

3. *What can you learn from Source C about the role of the 'Little ships' at Dunkirk?*

How was Britain able to survive Dunkirk?

In addition to lost and abandoned materials (see Source B), British forces lost almost 70,000 men killed or taken prisoner and the RAF lost almost 200 fighters during the evacuation of Dunkirk. Fighting in France continued for almost three weeks after the final evacuation. On 21 June 1940 the French government surrendered.

Source A: A table showing official figures for British and Allied troops landed after the evacuation from Dunkirk

Date	From the beaches (using the 'Little ships')	From Dunkirk harbour	Total
27 May		7,669	7,669
28 May	5,930	11,874	17,804
29 May	13,572	33,558	47,310
30 May	29,512	24,311	53,823
31 May	22,942	45,072	68,014
1 June	17,348	47,081	64,429
2 June	6,695	19,561	26,256
3 June	1,870	24,876	26,746
4 June	622	25,553	26,175
Total	98,491	239,555	338,226

Britain now stood alone against Nazi Germany. Churchill created the 'Dunkirk spirit', cleverly turning a military defeat into a propaganda victory by persuading the British people that the evacuation was a great success. The phrase 'Dunkirk spirit' then became synonymous with refusing to give up in time of crisis, which for Britain meant the duration of the war. Prime Minister Churchill was determined to continue the war and after Dunkirk he continued to make rousing and inspirational speeches to rally Britain. Churchill's speeches always explained why the war was being fought and why it was crucial to defeat Nazism. He ensured that the British people were united as one in the fight against Hitler.

Nevertheless, Churchill was always honest when he spoke. He said that wars were not won by retreating and that Dunkirk was 'Britain's greatest military defeat for many centuries'.

Source B: A table showing British army supplies used in France in 1939–40 and the supplies brought back to Britain from Dunkirk

	Shipped to France	Used in action	Destroyed or abandoned	Brought back
Guns	2,794		2,472	322
Vehicles	68,618		63,879	4,739
Motorcycles	21,081		20,548	533
Ammunition (tonnes)	109,000		76,697	32,303
Petrol (tonnes)	166,000		164,929	1,071

Source C: Part of a speech by Winston Churchill to Parliament, 4 June 1940, after the evacuation from Dunkirk

We shall go on to the end, we shall fight in France, we shall fight on the seas and oceans, we shall fight with growing confidence and growing strength in the air, we shall defend our island, whatever the cost may be, we shall fight on the beaches, we shall fight on the landing grounds, we shall fight in the fields and in the streets, we shall fight in the hills; we shall never surrender, and even if, which I do not for a moment believe, this island or a large part of it were subjugated and starving, then our Empire beyond the seas, armed and guarded by the British Fleet, would carry on the struggle, until, in God's good time, the New World, with all its power and might, steps forth to the rescue and the liberation of the Old.

Source D: A cartoon by David Low for the *Evening Standard*, 18 June 1940

'VERY WELL, ALONE'

Assistance from the USA

An additional crucial factor at this time that helped Britain to continue the war was its ability to trade with the USA and more importantly import food from the USA. Although the USA was neutral at this time, the American president, Franklin D. Roosevelt, sympathised with Britain and was prepared to give assistance. In September 1940, 55-year-old US warships were given to Britain in return for a lease on certain air and naval bases in the West Indies.

Eventually, of even greater significance was 'Lend Lease'. In March 1941, President Roosevelt persuaded Congress to 'lend' equipment to Britain during the duration of the war. This enabled Britain to get essential supplies from the USA and boosted the morale of the British people who no longer felt totally alone.

However, after Dunkirk, Hitler continued to prepare to invade Britain, naming his plan Operation Sealion. To be successful, Hitler needed control of the air. This was to be the next phase of the war – the aerial battle, which was to become known as the 'Battle of Britain', which took place over the summer months of 1940.

Tasks

1. Interview older teachers and relatives. Ask them what they think the 'Dunkirk spirit' means and how it originated.

2. Study Source A (page 35). What can you learn from Source A about the evacuation from Dunkirk? (Remember how to answer this type of question? For guidance, see page 12.)

3. What does Source B (page 35) show you about the military effects of Dunkirk on the British Army? (Remember how to answer this type of question? For guidance, see page 12.)

4. Study Source C (page 35). What was the purpose of Churchill's speech?

5. i) What message is the cartoonist putting over in Source D?

   ii) Devise your own caption for Source D.

6. Re-read pages 32–35. Select ten words that describe the way in which Winston Churchill encouraged the British people after he became Prime Minister.

7. Working in groups, choose either 'Dunkirk – Victory' or 'Dunkirk – Defeat' and present your case to the class.

Examination practice

This section provides guidance on how to answer the cross-referencing question from Unit 3, which is worth ten marks.

Question 1 – cross-referencing

Study Sources A, B and C. How far do Sources A, B and C support the view that Dunkirk was a victory for Britain? Explain your answer, using the sources.

Source A: From *1940: Myth and Reality*, Clive Ponting 1990. Ponting resigned from the British civil service after his trial under the Official Secrets Act in 1985. His history books offer controversial views

Once it was clear that the BEF was being evacuated, General Mason-Macfarlane, the Head of Military Intelligence, summoned journalists on 28 May and told them: 'I'm afraid there is going to be a considerable shock for the British public. It is your duty to act as shock-absorbers, so I have prepared ... a statement that can be published, subject to censorship.' The journalists were also told to blame the French for not fighting and to say that the BEF was undefeated; both statements were travesties of the truth. No news of the events at Dunkirk was released to the public until the 6p.m. BBC news on 30 May, five days after the evacuation had started and when nearly three-quarters of the BEF were already back in Britain. The public were then told, in a statement approved by the Ministry of Information, that 'men of the undefeated BEF have been coming home from France. They have not come back in triumph, they have come back in glory.'

Source B: From a radio broadcast by J. B. Priestley on 5 June 1940, the day after the evacuation from Dunkirk ended. Priestley was a popular British playwright and broadcaster whose talks were listened to by millions of people

Among those paddle steamers that will never return was one that I knew well, for it was the pride of our ferry service to the Isle of Wight ... And now never again will we board her at Cowes ... She has paddled and churned away – for ever. But now – look – this little steamer, like all her brave and battered sisters, is immortal. She'll go sailing proudly down the years in the epic of Dunkirk. And our great grand-children, when they learn how we began this war by snatching glory out of defeat, and then swept on to victory may also learn how the little holiday steamers made an excursion to hell and came back glorious.

Source C: From an article in the *New York Times*, 1 June 1940

So long as the English tongue survives, the word Dunkirk will be spoken with reverence. In that harbour, such a hell on earth as never blazed before, at the end of a lost battle, the rags and blemishes that had hidden the soul of democracy fell away. There, beaten but unconquered, in shining splendour, she faced the enemy, this shining thing in the souls of free men, which Hitler cannot command. It is in the great tradition of democracy. It is a future. It is victory.

How to answer

Use the planning grid on this page to help you to organise your answer and the flow chart on page 38 to show you how to construct your answer.

Source	Details that support the view	Details that do not support the view	Reliability of source	Extent of support
A				
B				
C				

STEP 1
- Make a note of any parts of Source A that support the view.
- Now explain any areas of support.

Example:
Source A supports the view because it suggests that Dunkirk was reported as a victory and that men had returned undefeated. The army was successful.

STEP 2
- Make a note of any parts of Source A that do not support the view.
- Now explain how it does not support the view.

Example:
Source A shows how the message of victory was created by military intelligence and that the journalists had to do as they were told.

STEP 3
- Make a note of the reliability of Source A.
- Now explain how this supports the view.

Example:
Source A provides reliable support for the view because it uses material from military intelligence and the Ministry of Information.

STEP 4
- Make a note of the unreliability of Source A.
- Now explain how this does not support the view.

Example:
Source A does not provide reliable support for the view because the author seeks to slant the view about Dunkirk against the government.

STEP 5
- Now make a judgement on how much Source A supports the view.
- Use judgement words or phrases such as 'it strongly supports', 'it provides little support', 'there is some support'.

Example:
Source A does offer some support for the view because the BBC gave a statement about the evacuation but it is evident that the media was being controlled and that any news had been vetted.

STEP 6
Now repeat steps 1–5 for Sources B and C, but plan your answer for each source first, using the planning grid on page 37.

Have a go yourself

STEP 7
Write a conclusion for all three sources. This should begin with the word 'Overall' and make a final judgement on how much the three sources support the view. Remember to use judgement words/phrases.

Have a go yourself

The Battle of Britain

Source A: A table showing different figures for German losses during the Battle of Britain			
Date	**RAF claim in 1940**	**RAF claim post-war**	**German High Command**
15 August 1940	185	76	55
18 August 1940	155	71	49
15 September 1940	185	56	50
27 September 1940	153	55	42
Totals	678	258	196

Tasks

1. *Study Source A. Why was the RAF claim greater in 1940 than after the war?*

2. *Why was the German claim less than that of the British?*

After the defeat of France in June 1940, Hitler began planning an invasion of Britain. However, in order to carry out the invasion, the German air force, the *Luftwaffe*, had to gain control of the air by destroying the Royal Air Force (RAF). During August and early September 1940, the RAF and *Luftwaffe* fought for control of the air over the skies of Britain. The outcome of the battle was decisive for Britain's survival.

This chapter answers the following questions:

- What happened during the Battle of Britain?
- Why was the RAF successful?
- What was the importance of the Battle of Britain?

Examination skills
In this chapter you will be given further guidance on how to answer the cross-referencing question, which is worth ten marks.

What happened during the Battle of Britain?

Hitler did not really want war with Britain. He felt that Britain was his natural ally, not his enemy. However, Churchill made it clear that he would not make a deal with Germany and that Britain would fight to the finish. So for this reason, Hitler decided to attack Britain during August and early September 1940.

Hitler's *Blitzkrieg* tactics that had worked so well against France (see page 33) could not work across the Channel. To conquer Britain would require a sea and air invasion. However, Hitler's military advisers made it clear that any such invasion would fail if German forces were attacked by the British RAF and navy. The German navy was no match for the British navy. Nevertheless, the military advisers believed that if the RAF could be wiped out, then the British naval dockyards could be destroyed by *Luftwaffe* bombing. This would result in the loss of British sea power – allowing a German sea-borne invasion of Britain, known as Operation Sealion, to take place.

> ### Source A: Churchill's broadcast to the nation, 18 June 1940
>
> *The Battle of France is over. I expect that the Battle of Britain is about to begin. Upon this battle depends the survival of Christian civilisation and our own British life. The whole fury and might of the enemy must soon be turned on us. Hitler knows that he will have to break this Island or lose the war. If we can stand up to him all Europe may be free. But if we fail, the whole world will sink into the abyss of a new Dark Age.*

Key events of battle

The Battle of Britain was not a single battle but a series of air battles in August and early September 1940, as the diary below shows.

1 August Hitler gave his order: 'Using all possible means, the German air force will smash the British air force in as little time as possible.'

2 August Goering issued the orders for Adlertag or Eagle Day, the destruction of the RAF.

12 August The *Luftwaffe* attacked the south coast, more especially the docks and war industries of Portsmouth and Southampton and the **radar station** on the Isle of Wight.

15 August The largest attack so far with five successive waves of German attacks and over 2000 **sorties**, two-thirds of them by fighter planes. However, the *Luftwaffe* was unable to catch the RAF planes on the ground refuelling and rearming. The Germans nicknamed this 'Black Thursday' because they suffered heavy losses including 69 aircraft and 190 crew. The RAF lost 34 aircraft and 13 pilots.

30 August The *Luftwaffe* now changed its strategy to the destruction of the RAF **sector stations** in the South-East. One such station, Biggin Hill, suffered the first of six major attacks.

1–6 September The *Luftwaffe* attacked the sector stations. In the first six days of September the *Luftwaffe* lost 125 planes but the British losses were also heavy – 119 aircraft and the RAF reserve of experienced fighting crew was running low. The position looked grim and Britain seemed close to defeat.

7 September Hitler made a big mistake. He switched from bombing the fighter plane bases and the sector stations of Kent to the bombing of London. This gave the RAF a vital breathing space. The pressure was taken off the battered sector stations.

15 September The decisive battle took place when the *Luftwaffe* made its supreme effort with an all-out assault on London in daylight. The Germans lost 56 planes and called off their attempt to destroy the RAF.

17 September Hitler decided to postpone Operation Sealion.

Source B: B. J. Ellan, a Spitfire pilot, describes what he saw on 15 September

I saw above the black specks a tangle of white condensation trails – the whole sky ahead seemed filled with aircraft. As we got closer I recognised the bombers as Dorniers, about thirty in each formation stretching away towards the coast. Above the bombers weaved Me 109s. Never before, or since, have I seen so many enemy aircraft. There were hundreds of them! It was an amazing sight and one which I shall remember all my life.

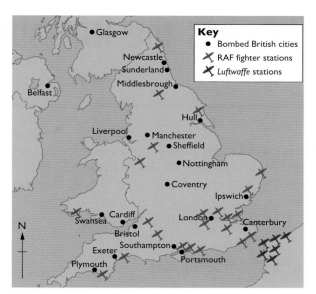

A map showing the fighter stations and cities attacked by the *Luftwaffe* during the Battle of Britain and the Blitz

Source C: A photograph of fighter pilots racing for their Spitfires in what was known as 'scrambling', during the Battle of Britain

Tasks

1. *How useful are Sources A and C as evidence of the Battle of Britain? (Remember how to answer this type of question? For guidance, see pages 68–70.)*

2. *Why did the* Luftwaffe *decide to attack the RAF in 1940?*

3. *Which were the decisive days in the Battle of Britain?*

4. *Study Source B. What can you learn from Source B about the Battle of Britain? (Remember how to answer this type of question? For guidance, see page 12.)*

5. *The British government would often use photographs, such as Source C, for propaganda purposes. Devise a suitable propaganda caption for the photograph.*

Why was the RAF successful?

Hermann Goering, head of the *Luftwaffe*, had been confident of success in the Battle of Britain. He seemed to have more high-quality aircraft than the British, especially the Messerschmitt 109 fighter plane and bombers such as the Heinkel III and the Junker Ju 88. He also had more well-trained pilots. However, the British victory was due to the strengths of the RAF and the weaknesses of the *Luftwaffe*.

Luftwaffe weaknesses

A German Stuka dive-bomber

- Goering, the commander of the *Luftwaffe*, had little understanding of tactics. He underestimated the strength of the RAF, especially the fighter planes, and often sent German bomber planes unescorted.
- The German fighter planes could only carry limited fuel and could not fly over Britain long enough to protect the German bombers. These flew unescorted to bomb London on the decisive day of the battle, 15 September 1940, when 56 German bombers were lost.
- The Germans had to fight over Britain and lost far more pilots who were difficult to replace. Once the plane was shot down, the German pilots were either killed or captured.
- Hitler made the mistake of switching their attacks on 7 September, just when the RAF was running out of fighter planes.

RAF strengths

A British Spitfire

- British planes were often in the skies and above the German planes as they arrived over Britain.
- The two British fighter planes, the Hurricane and Spitfire, were a good match for their German counterpart, the Messerschmitt 109.
- In the mid-1930s, the British had developed a sophisticated defence system against enemy bombing known as radar. Radar stations made it possible to track German planes and so to concentrate the defence just where it was needed. The British had sector stations that acted as a nerve centre collecting the information from radar and sending the fighter planes to intercept the German planes.
- The British had a very accomplished and experienced commander in Air Chief Marshall Dowding, nicknamed 'Stuffy' because of his lack of humour, who made effective use of radar and the sector stations.
- The British were fighting over their own territory. This meant that British pilots that were shot down could be sent back into combat.

The inside of a radar station in 1940. Radar station operators were able to detect the position and direction of German aircraft using signals from radio waves that showed up on a screen

Source A: The memories of Theodor Plotte, who was part of the crew of a Stuka dive-bomber

We were in Normandy, France, and from there we flew the Stukas to England. While I was based there we lost 85 planes shot down over England and the Channel. Later on the crews mutinied. They didn't want to fight any more because their planes could not compete with the Hurricanes and Spitfires.

Source B: From *Fighter*, written by Len Deighton in 1977

The most common type of attack was a dive out of the sun, pulling out behind and under the tail of the enemy, and firing while in his blind spot.

Tasks

1. *What reasons do Sources A and B suggest for the RAF victory in the Battle of Britain?*

2. *How useful are Sources A and B as evidence of the Battle of Britain? Explain your answer, using Sources A and B and your own knowledge. (For guidance on answering this type of question, see pages 68–70.)*

3. *Working in pairs, produce a mind map placing the reasons for the RAF victory in the Battle of Britain in order of importance:*
   * *move clockwise beginning with the most important at 12 o'clock*
   * *give reasons for your choice of most important reason.*

What was the importance of the Battle of Britain?

The Battle of Britain was seen as a very important turning point in the Second World War.

- It was Hitler's first real defeat and showed that, although the German armed forces were very effective in *Blitzkrieg* warfare with fast-moving tactics, they were beatable when faced with a long drawn-out conflict.
- It was a great morale booster for the British people, especially during the **Blitz** of 1940–41 (see pages 47–57). Britain was saved from invasion, at least for the time being, as Hitler postponed Operation Sealion.
- It made Britain more attractive as a future ally of the USA and encouraged Roosevelt to give material assistance. Roosevelt sympathised with Britain and agreed to 'Lend Lease' by which the USA was prepared to 'lend' equipment to Britain for the duration of the war.
- It was an important reason for the survival of Britain alone in the years 1940–41 when the *Luftwaffe* turned their attention to bombing Britain out the war in the Blitz of 1940–41.

However, it may not have been a decisive turning point in the war.

- The *Luftwaffe* had failed in their attempt to destroy the RAF but Hitler's armies had not been defeated.

- Even if the RAF had been defeated, the British navy might have been strong enough to prevent a subsequent German invasion.

Source A: **A poster issued by the British government immediately after the battle**

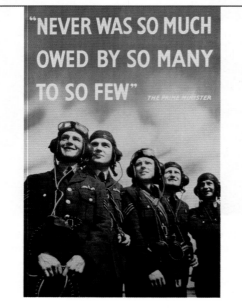

Source B: **From a radio broadcast by Winston Churchill, 20 August 1940**

The gratitude of every home in our Island, in our Empire, and indeed throughout the world, except in the homes of the guilty, goes out to the British airmen who, undaunted by the odds, unwearied in their constant challenge and mortal danger, are turning the tide of the World War by their prowess and by their devotion. Never in the field of human conflict was so much owed by so many to so few. All hearts go out to the fighter pilots, whose brilliant actions we see with our own eyes day after day.

Tasks

1. *Study Source A and use your own knowledge. What was the purpose of this poster? Use details from the poster and your own knowledge to explain your answer. (Remember how to answer this type of question? For guidance, see page 20.)*

2. *How reliable is Source B as evidence of the Battle of Britain?*

War and the Transformation of British Society 1931–1951

Examination practice

This section provides guidance on how to answer the cross-referencing question from Unit 3, which is worth ten marks.

Question 1 – cross-referencing

Study Sources A, B and C. How far do Sources A and B support the view of Source C about the Battle of Britain? Explain your answer, using the sources.

Source A: From the memories of Group Captain Peter Matthews

I remember the attack we made on a big formation – we went in head-on. We wanted to get higher and avoid any fighters and shoot down the bombers from that position, but we couldn't gain the height in time. So we made a head-on attack on a bunch of Me 110s – we were very successful and shot down three or four. Our Hurricanes weren't as fast as the Germans but we were more manoeuvrable. But those Hurricanes took a hell of a punishment and we did lose one of our planes.

Source B: A painting showing British and German planes in the Battle of Britain, 1940

Source C: From the memories of Oberleutnant Hans Gollnisch

We headed for London, escorted by hundreds of German fighters. The targets were the docks which could already be seen when we were hit by a very short burst of fire from the machine guns of the RAF fighters that had approached from below and behind, unseen by the escorting fighters. Our plane was badly damaged and the situation was grim. I had no alternative but to make a difficult landing. We got down in one piece, set fire to our plane and gave ourselves up to the police and soldiers.

How to answer

Use the planning grid on this page to help you to organise your answer and the flow chart on page 46 to show you how to construct your answer.

Source	Details that are similar	Details that differ	Reliability of source	Extent of support
A				
B				
C				

STEP 1
- Make a note of any parts of Source A that are similar to Source C.
- Now explain any areas of support.

Example:
Source A supports Source C because both sources suggest that the RAF were successful in shooting down German planes during the Battle of Britain.

STEP 2
- Make a note of any parts of Source A that do not support Source C.
- Now explain any areas of difference.

Example:
Source A suggests that the British fighters were not totally successful and lost one Hurricane whereas Source C mentions only German losses.

STEP 3
- Make a note of the reliability of Source A.
- Now explain how this supports Source C.

Example:
Source A provides reliable support for Source C because it is an eyewitness account from a British pilot who took part in the Battle of Britain.

STEP 4
- Make a note of the unreliability of Source A.
- Now explain how this does not support Source C.

Example:
Source A does not provide reliable support for Source C because it may be giving a one-sided view of the battle in order to glorify the role of the RAF.

STEP 5
- Now make a judgement on how much Source A supports Source C.
- Use judgement words or phrases such as 'it strongly supports', 'it provides little support', 'there is some support'.

Example:
Source A gives strong support to the views of Source C as both are eyewitness accounts of the battle that suggest British success.

STEP 6
Now repeat steps 1 to 5 for Source B.

Have a go yourself

STEP 7
Write a conclusion for all three sources. This should begin with the word 'Overall' and make a final judgement on how much Sources A and B support Source C. Remember to use judgement words/phrases.

Have a go yourself

The Blitz

Source A: A British poster of 1940

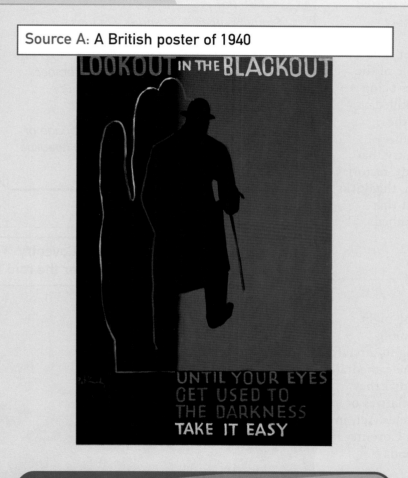

LOOKOUT IN THE BLACKOUT

UNTIL YOUR EYES
GET USED TO
THE DARKNESS
TAKE IT EASY

From September 1940, Hitler changed tactics and decided to try to bomb Britain into submission. This became known as the Blitz. During the period of September 1940 to May 1941, the *Luftwaffe* bombed Britain's major towns and cities. The British government brought in various measures to deal with the Blitz including the **blackout**, **air raid shelters** and the **Home Guard**. Having survived this first Blitz, the British were then attacked by Hitler's revenge weapons, the V-1 and V-2 bombs, in 1944–45.

This chapter answers the following questions:

- What were the effects of the Blitz of 1940–41?
- What measures were taken to deal with the Blitz?
- What were the key features of evacuation?
- What were the effects of the second Blitz, 1944–45?

Task

Study Source A and use your own knowledge.
Why was this poster published? Use details from the poster and your own knowledge to explain your answer.
(Remember how to answer this type of question? For guidance, see page 20.)

Examination skills
This chapter provides an opportunity to practise some of the question types from Unit 3.

What were the effects of the Blitz of 1940–41?

The bombing of Britain known as the Blitz began after Hitler gave up his attempt to invade Britain in September 1940 (see page 40). Hitler started the Blitz because he:

- was trying to force Britain to surrender. The Blitz was really intended to break the morale of the British people. If they saw their homes being destroyed and their loved ones being killed, Hitler believed that they would force the government to come to terms with him.
- wanted to destroy transport and industry that helped the war effort, such as shipyards, factories and railways. For example, in London, the docks were attacked regularly and this meant that people in the East End were often bombed.

The German attacks

Coventry

Coventry suffered its worst attack on the night of 14 November 1940, being hit by 30,000 **incendiary bombs**, with the target being its aircraft factories. Much of the city, including the cathedral, was destroyed. People were so terrified that they fled the city each night, sleeping with relatives or in farmers' barns or camping in open fields. Yet, in spite of this savage raid, the factories in Coventry were back in full production within five days.

> **Tasks**
>
> 1. *Study Sources A, B and C. Do these sources support the view that the German attack on Coventry was very effective? Explain your answer, using the sources. (Remember how to answer this type of question? For guidance, see pages 37–38.)*
>
> 2. *Imagine Source D was on the front page of a British newspaper. Create your own headline for this photo.*

Source B: A street in the centre of Coventry near the cathedral the morning after the raid

Source A: A broadcast from German radio, 16 November 1940, on the raid on Coventry

More than 500 planes took part in the greatest attack in the history of aerial warfare. About 500 tonnes of high explosives and 30,000 incendiary bombs were dropped. In a short time all large and small factories were set on fire. The German air force has struck a violent blow at British civilian morale.

Source C: From the *Daily Herald*, 16 November 1940

So the orgy began. Bombs by the thousand were poured on houses, churches, shops and hotels. Squadron after squadron dived on the helpless city. What has it achieved? It has proved once again the calm courage of ordinary British people. It has fortified their resolve to fight on.

Other attacks

The North-West, and Manchester in particular, was attacked in December 1940. Liverpool was attacked regularly and on 3 May 1941 suffered the biggest single raid on a mainland city, involving over 600 bombers. The city lost some of its finest buildings, with fires burning out of control because water mains were hit. A freighter, the SS *Malakand*, carrying 1000 tonnes of explosives, received a direct hit. The docks around the ship and the nearby packed terraced homes were devastated. Other notable targets included Hull, Plymouth, Bristol and Birmingham. Glasgow and the Clyde shipyards were hit hard in the spring of 1941. Belfast was devastated in April and May 1941– at least 1000 people were killed in the city and 150,000 made homeless.

London

London was the primary target for the German bombings, especially the East End with its docks and factories. Between 2 September and 2 November 1940 London was bombed every night. The House of Commons building was destroyed and Buckingham Palace damaged. King George VI and Queen Elizabeth (the late Queen Mother) were often on the scene soon after a severe raid to cheer and encourage people as they struggled to save those trapped under the debris. Over 15,000 people were killed and 250,000 made homeless. These raids continued through 1941 with the worst on 10 May when thousands were left without electricity, gas and water.

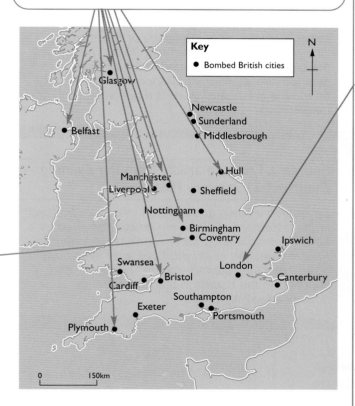

Source D: **Damage to a street in south-west London, 17 October 1940. The bomb also destroyed the sub-surface gas, electricity and water mains and caused flooding in the underground station**

The effects of the Blitz

The Blitz did less damage than many people had expected. It did not destroy the morale of the population. If anything, it made those affected even more determined to support the war. It did not greatly reduce the production of factories, and damage to transport was quickly repaired. However, over 3 million homes were destroyed, 60,000 were killed and there is evidence of some damage to morale.

Source E: From Hitler's war directive against England, 6 February 1941

The bombing campaign has had the least effect of all, so far as we can see, on the morale and will to resist of the English people. No decisive success can be expected from terror attacks on residential areas.

Source F: An extract from a local government report on the East End of London, September 1940

The whole story of last weekend has been one of unplanned hysteria. The newspaper versions of life going on normally in the East End are greatly distorted. There was no bread, no milk, no telephones. There is no humour or laughter. There was thus every excuse for people to be distressed. There was no understanding in the huge government buildings of central London for the tiny crumbled streets of massed populations.

Source G: Extracts from the diary of Joseph Goebbels, the Nazi Minister of Propaganda

11 October 1940 We shall be able to force England to her knees during the next few weeks.

12 October 1940 Horrific reports from London. A capital city on the slide. An international drama without parallel, but we must see it through.

23 October 1940 We shall battle on remorselessly to destroy their last hope.

1 November 1940 The Führer intends to keep hammering England until they break.

Source H: A German radio report, 18 September 1940

The legend of British self-control and coolness under fire is being destroyed. All reports from London agree in stating that the people are seized by fear – hair-raising fear. The 7 million Londoners have completely lost their self-control. They run aimlessly about the streets and are victims of bombs and bursting shells.

Source I: An extract from an official report into the effects of the bombing of Portsmouth, January 1941

By 6.00p.m. all traffic is moving northwards. The movement begins at 3.30p.m. and continues until dusk. The people are making for the bridge on the main road out of Portsmouth in order to sleep in the northern suburbs, the surrounding hills, or towns and villages in the radius of twenty miles. One night it was estimated that 90,000 people left the city. Looting and wanton destruction have reached almost alarming proportions. The effect on morale is bad and there is a general feeling of desperation.

Source J: From an article from the *Evening Standard*, 13 January 1941

Seventeen women and children who were trapped in the basement of a London house damaged by a bomb last night shouted to wardens who went to their rescue: 'We're alright. Look after everybody else'. Then they started singing 'Tipperary' and shouting to the people in the road. 'Are we downhearted? No'.

Source K: **A photograph of a market stall open for business in London after a bombing raid**

Tasks

3. *Study Source E. What can you learn from Source E about the effects of the Blitz? (Remember how to answer this type of question? For guidance, see page 12.)*

4. *How useful are Sources H and I as evidence of the effects of the Blitz? Explain your answer, using Sources H and I and your own knowledge. (For guidance on answering this type of question, see pages 68–70.)*

5. *Study Source K and use your own knowledge. What was the purpose of this photograph? Use details from the photograph and your own knowledge to explain your answer. (Remember how to answer this type of question? For guidance, see page 20.)*

6. *Working in pairs, make a copy of and complete the following table. One example has been done for you.*

Sources that suggest the Blitz was not a success	Sources that suggest the Blitz was a success
Source J suggests that morale was high as people were singing.	

7. *Study Sources E–K and use your own knowledge. 'The Blitz of 1940–41 was successful in lowering the morale of the British people.' How far do these sources support this statement? Use details from the sources and your own knowledge to explain your answer. (For guidance on answering this type of question, see pages 96–98.)*

What measures were taken to deal with the Blitz?

The government introduced a series of measures to deal with the Blitz including air raid shelters, the Home Guard and the blackout.

Air raid shelters

The government supplied its citizens with air raid shelters. The first shelters, known as Anderson shelters, were delivered in February 1939. Altogether, 400,000 Anderson air raid shelters were distributed. These were dug into the garden and covered with earth. They were designed to protect people against falling brickwork if the houses were bombed. In areas where it was impossible to use Anderson shelters, large concrete shelters with curved roofs were constructed.

Source A: An Anderson shelter

However, Anderson shelters were not popular because they meant sleeping outside. Some people used Morrison shelters, which were given out in 1941. These were steel cages, which fitted under a dining table with enough room to fit two adults and two small children.

Many people, however, had no shelters, particularly those living in city centres or in flats. Some people moved in with friends or relatives during raids and others moved onto the ground floor. Here, or sometimes in a cellar, they constructed a safe room.

Source B: A photograph of a two-tiered Morrison shelter from a government catalogue of 1942. It was described as the ultimate in comfort and luxury and was given free to poorer families

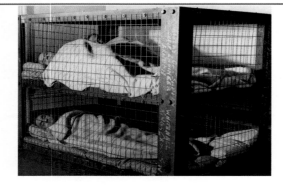

When the raids became serious in the second week of September 1940, people began to try to force their way into underground stations in London. At first the government did not allow the underground stations to be used as shelters. It wanted to ensure that the trains could be used for transport. However, the early attacks were so severe and so damaging to morale that the decision was reversed. One of the first stations to be opened was Bethnal Green in the East End.

The shelters were often packed. Children queued in the afternoon in order to stake a claim to a patch of platform for the family. A white line was drawn 2.5 metres from the edge of the platform. This was to let passengers reach the train. At 7.30p.m. the line was moved to 1.2 metres from the edge. That was the last chance to find a bed space. Latecomers slept in the passages or on the stairs. Electricity to lines was switched off at 10.30p.m. and adults would sleep in the fifth bay between the lines. People preferred the underground stations as a shelter because they could socialise with other families and share a common threat. In addition, voluntary services began to provide hot drinks.

Despite all of these precautions, it was still estimated that 60 per cent of Londoners stayed in their own homes throughout the Blitz.

Source C: **A photograph of children sleeping in an underground station**

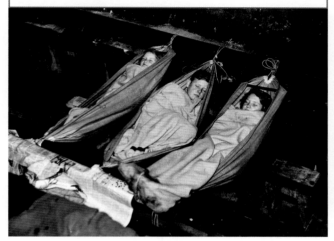

Source E: **A photograph of fishermen on Holy Island, off the coast of Northumberland. They are learning how to use rifles as part of their Home Guard training**

Source D: **An interview with a Londoner who remembers the Blitz**

People would rush to get to the tubes, almost knock you down to get to the escalator. We lived like rats underground. People spread newspapers on the floor to show it was their territory. Sometimes you'd get people squaring up and fights.

The Home Guard

The Local Defence Volunteers (LDV) was set up in July 1940, but the name was changed almost immediately to the Home Guard, and became known as 'Dad's Army'. It was mostly made up of older men, often former soldiers. It called for men aged 17 to 65 to volunteer. On the first day 250,000 were recruited. At first units had no uniforms and few weapons, but they eventually became more organised. It trained at night and at weekends.

The Home Guard's main role was to take over duties from the regular army. It patrolled beaches, stood sentry duty at nights and weekends and even rounded up German pilots after they were shot down. Home Guard battalions were also trained to carry on a **guerrilla war** after a German invasion and secret hideouts were constructed.

Tasks

1. *Using evidence from Sources A and B, explain why many people preferred to use the Morrison rather than the Anderson shelter.*

2. *Study Source B and use your own knowledge. What was the purpose of this photograph? Use details from the photograph and your own knowledge to explain your answer. (Remember how to answer this type of question? For guidance, see page 20.)*

3. *Study Source C. The government would often use photographs like this to keep up the morale of the people during the Blitz. Write a morale-raising caption to go with this photograph.*

4. *Study Source D. What can you learn from Source D about the underground during the Blitz? (Remember how to answer this type of question? For guidance, see page 12.)*

5. *What does Source E suggest about the age range of the Home Guard?*

The blackout

The blackout had the most immediate effect on people. It was introduced so that German bombers could not see cities from the air, therefore making bombing more difficult. People had to ensure that no light was visible from their homes. Failure to do so would mean a visit from an **air raid warden**. Streetlights were not lit and cars had to be driven without lights. This led to many accidents. In December 1939, over 1500 people were killed on British roads. This was nearly three times the pre-war level. Many people fell into canals or from railway station platforms.

Restrictions were eased later in the war so that dimmed torches could be used in streets and drivers could use dimmed headlights. To assist pedestrians and drivers, kerbs and roadsides were painted black and white. The government realised that a lighted cigarette could not be seen from an aeroplane and people were allowed to smoke at night, although they were not allowed to strike a match in the street. Torches had to be covered with tissue paper and pointed downwards.

Source F: From an interview given in 1940

It was inky black. I had no torch and there was not a glimmer of light. I could not see where the water was. I groped along the bushes for ten minutes. I was frankly terrified. In the end I went down on my hands and knees and crawled all the way home. I met two people crawling the other way.

Tasks

6. *What does Source G suggest about government preparations for the blackout?*

7. *How useful are Sources F and H as evidence of the effects of the blackout? Explain your answer, using Sources F and H and your own knowledge. (For guidance on answering this type of question, see pages 68–70.)*

8. *Working in pairs, think of five suggestions for ways in which people could cope with the blackout during the Second World War.*

Source G: A photograph taken in 1939 showing people painting white circles on trees and curbs to assist road users during the blackout

Source H: A photograph of two boys in 1941. The boys have white paper pinned to their backs so they can be seen as they walk along roads after blackout time

What were the key features of evacuation?

A group of children wave and cheer as they are evacuated from London to Devon

The government expected that the Germans would attack Britain from the air, so it took precautions to protect its civilians from bombings. Children were to be protected by being moved from the likeliest targets, the cities, to the countryside where it was thought they would be safe.

Organisation

The **evacuation** began on 1 September 1939, the day that Hitler invaded Poland. Although many parents were reluctant to be separated from their children they accepted they would be safer in the country. Parents were told what the children needed to take with them and where they were to assemble for evacuation. Many city schools were closed and teachers went with the children to the countryside to carry on teaching them. Over 1 million were evacuated.

At their destinations the evacuees gathered in village or school halls where they were chosen by the foster family they were to live with. Homesickness and the 'Phoney War' (see page 30), when little fighting took place and there were no enemy bombing raids, saw many children drift back to the cities by Christmas 1939.

When German bombers began blitzing London in 1940, a second evacuation from the cities took place. There was a further wave of evacuations in 1944, when the Germans used their V-1 flying bombs and V-2 missiles to bomb Britain (see page 57).

Source A: The memories of an evacuee

Everything was so clean in our room. We were given flannels and toothbrushes. We'd never cleaned our teeth until then. Hot water came from the tap and there was a lavatory upstairs. This was all rather odd and scary.

Was evacuation a success?

- Evacuation saved many lives.
- There is evidence that some people tried to avoid taking evacuees.
- The organisation of the evacuation was criticised as children would arrive in village halls where they were 'chosen' by their host families, almost like cattle at a market.
- The organisation was sometimes poor, especially the way in which the evacuees were lined up in village halls and inspected by their host families. Clean looking girls were the most popular because they could do domestic chores followed by strong looking boys who could work on the farm. Dirty or unattractive children were left until last.
- Evacuees were not used to rural life and there was a clash between city and country values. Evacuees often found themselves in much wealthier homes. Host families had to cope with different standards of behaviour with some children from poorer homes lacking proper toilet and table manners. Some urinated on newspapers and used their fingers rather than knives and forks to eat their food. Others arrived with diseases and lice and wet their beds.
- A number of evacuees were homesick. They missed their own families, far away in the cities, and found the countryside boring. During evacuation children were sometimes split up from their brothers and sisters.
- Some children from poor inner city areas saw the countryside for the first time, more especially green fields, orchards and farm animals.
- Many evacuees stayed with better-off people and were given a better standard of living including a healthier diet, fresh air and walks in the countryside. Some found it difficult to adjust to their old way of life when they returned home after evacuation.
- Evacuation showed better-off people in the countryside the social problems of families living in inner-city areas and increased the demand for change.
- Some evacuees experienced bullying by children who already lived in the countryside and resented these intruders from the cities who were causing overcrowding in schools.
- Some foster parents did not treat the evacuees well, beating them and not giving them enough food. Some saw the children as a burden.
- During the 'Phoney War' (see page 30), many children drifted back to the cities by Christmas 1939 and had to be evacuated again once the Blitz began.

Source B: The evacuation memories of the film actor Michael Caine

My brother Clarence and I used to sleep together and poor Clarence used to wet his bed because he was a nervous kid. Our foster mother could never tell who'd done it so she used to bash the daylights out of both of us. So, of course, the more Clarence got hit the more he wet the bed. It was then that we started to get locked in the cupboard.

Source C: A middle-class girl who lived in the countryside of Northern Ireland remembers her experience of evacuees from Belfast

They are all filthy and the smell of the room is terrible. They refuse all food except tea and bread. They make puddles all over the floor.

Task

Make a copy of the following table. Complete the table using Sources A (page 55), B and C and the text on pages 55–56. One example has been done for you.

Successes of evacuation	Limitations of evacuation
	Source B suggests that some evacuees were treated badly.

What were the effects of the second Blitz, 1944–45?

In 1944 and 1945 Britain was attacked from the air once again. These were from Hitler's 'Vengeance' weapons known as the V-1 and V-2.

Name of weapon	Description	Damage it caused	How serious a threat?
V-1, nicknamed the doodlebug because of the noise it made while in flight.	Pilot-less rocket planes. These could be launched from railway trucks, which were moved from place to place. Each rocket carried about 1 tonne of explosive and when it ran out of fuel it fell to the ground and exploded. V-1s flew at about 560 kilometres per hour and could be shot down, but the resulting explosion could be very dangerous. One Mosquito, the fastest RAF plane at the time, had all its paint stripped off after shooting one down.	Just over 10,000 V-1s were launched against England from the coast of France but only 3500 of these found a target, killing 6200 people. The rest were shot down or crashed before reaching the coast.	The V-1 did, at first, affect the morale of the people of London who had not experienced the Blitz for three years. They were an unknown weapon that could fall anywhere without prior warning, except that the doodlebug noise stopped shortly before the rocket fell to the ground. However, the V-1 threat was not too serious because the British installed anti-aircraft guns along the south coast and used fighter planes to intercept them. Some pilots attempted to bring the V-1s down over open country by flying alongside them and tipping them over with the end of their wing. This upset the balance of the V-1, which was controlled by a gyroscope. The V-1 originally had fixed launch sites in France and Holland that were targets for Allied bombing raids. The Allies overran the launch sites once they advanced out of Normandy in the second half of 1944 and early 1945.

Name of weapon	Description	Damage it caused	How serious a threat?
V-2	They were real rockets, which were fired from sites in Holland. They could not be shot down and there was no defence against them. The V-2 carried only a slightly bigger explosive load of 1000 kilograms than the V-1.	From September 1944 until the end of March 1945 an average of five a day fell on England, killing nearly 3000 civilians.	V-2s were a much more serious threat than V-1s because they could not be stopped as they reached a speed of 4000 kilometres per hour on impact. They exploded without warning. The attacks were only stopped when the launch sites were overrun by the advancing Allied armies in 1945. Fortunately, Hitler developed this weapon too late in the war to cause serious damage.

Task

Which was the greater threat to Britain, the V-1 or the V-2? Give reasons for your answer.

Key Topic 3: Britain at War

Source A: A Ministry of Agriculture poster issued in 1941. The green symbol in the bottom left was the 'Dig for Victory' sign

Task

What does Source A tell us about the role of the government in the Second World War?

This key topic examines Britain at war, not only on the Home Front but also its contribution to the defeat of Germany from D-Day in June 1944 to the end of hostilities in May 1945. It starts by looking in detail at the role of government during the war and how the difficult problems of food supplies and rationing were dealt with. There is then an analysis of the contribution of women during the war and the effect this had on changing their role. Finally, the reasons for the success of D-Day are considered along with the other reasons for the defeat of Germany.

Each chapter explains a key issue and examines important lines of enquiry as outlined below.

Chapter 7: The role of government, food supplies and rationing (pages 59–70)
- What was the role of government during the war?
- How important were censorship and propaganda?
- What was the impact of the war on food supplies?

Chapter 8: The changing role of women (pages 71–76)
- What contribution did women make to the war effort?
- What effects did women's contribution to the war have on the position of women, 1945–51?

Chapter 9: D-Day and the defeat of Germany (pages 77–87)
- Why did the Allies invade Normandy in 1944 and how did they prepare for it?
- What were the events of D-Day, 6 June 1944?
- What advances were made by the Allies in the West, 1944–45?
- What developments took place on the Eastern Front, 1943–45?
- What other reasons contributed to the defeat of Germany?

The role of government, food supplies and rationing

Source A: **A British government poster, 1942**

'The South Downs'

your **BRITAIN** · *fight for it now*

ISSUED BY A.B.C.A

Task

Study Source A and use your own knowledge. What was the purpose of this poster? Use details from the poster and your own knowledge to explain your answer. (Remember how to answer this type of question? For guidance, see page 20.)

Although war had been on the horizon for several years, when it did break out in 1939, it was a shock to the British people. Most citizens could remember the horrors of the First World War and how it changed their everyday lives. They knew how the government had taken greater control of such things as industry, transport and, by the end of the war, food distribution. Unlike the First World War, in the Second World War the government introduced rationing almost immediately. A new ministry was set up to look after propaganda and censorship and it became almost impossible to escape the hand of the government. Most crucial of all was the introduction of rationing of food and clothing, something that affected everyone and became a source of irritation throughout the war and after.

This chapter answers the following questions:

- What was the role of government during the war?
- How important were censorship and propaganda?
- What was the impact of the war on food supplies?

Examination skills
In this chapter you will be given guidance on how to answer the utility question, which is worth ten marks.

What was the role of government during the war?

As the threat of war approached in the summer of 1939, the British government introduced the Emergency Powers (Defence) Act 1939. This was passed on 24 August and it allowed the British government to take up emergency powers to:

- secure public safety
- defend the realm
- maintain supplies and services essential to the life of the country
- carry out the war effectively.

The Act gave the government wide powers, without reference to parliament, to create regulations that covered almost every aspect of everyday life in the country.

In order to carry these powers out the Prime Minister, Neville Chamberlain, created five new ministries:

- Home Security (attached to the Home Office)
- Information
- Shipping
- Economic Warfare
- Food.

In addition, much British industry and transport was taken over by the government.

You have already seen that the government began the evacuation of over 1 million children before the official outbreak of war (see pages 55–56). Once fighting had started, it soon became clear that the government would use the act extensively and, in doing so, radically alter the relationship between the people and government.

Source A: **A poster published by the Ministry of Information during the Second World War**

you never know who's listening!

CARELESS TALK COSTS LIVES

Tasks

1. *What does Source A tell us about the work of the Ministry of Information?*

2. *Look at the five new ministries created by Chamberlain. Write one sentence to explain why you think each was created.*

How important were censorship and propaganda?

Source A: **The censor's office, Liverpool, November 1939. Many of the workers could speak several languages**

The government was aware that it had to ensure that people would support the war at all costs and tried to shape their ideas. It was hoped that by constant persuasion and suggestion people's attitudes would be positively influenced. Moreover, existing ideas and beliefs would be strengthened. The government tried to achieve these aims by means of **propaganda**.

In addition, the government wanted to ensure that information would not be given away to the enemy, or given to the British people that might damage morale. This meant introducing **censorship**.

There was censorship on overseas mail (see Source B) and the government examined all letters going abroad. If there was any sensitive material in the mail, it could be blacked out, cut out or returned to the sender. Soldiers' letters home were subject to censorship to ensure that military secrets were not inadvertently given away. Telephone calls were also subject to censorship (even King George and Winston Churchill faced this restriction).

Certain items of news were not broadcast or published because the Ministry of Information thought they would damage the morale of the people. On occasions, photographs were not published because they were felt to be too distressing and would reduce enthusiasm for the war effort (see Source C, page 62).

Newspapers were carefully monitored, but there was only one case of closing down the press. This was in January 1941, when the Communist newspaper the *Daily Worker* was banned because it supported Stalin and continually attacked the British government and its leaders with rarely any condemnation of Hitler.

Source B: **A letter that was returned to the sender by the censor**

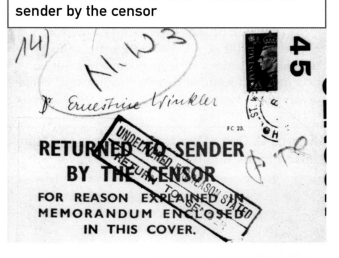

Task

1. *How useful are Sources A and B as evidence of censorship during the war? Explain your answer, using Sources A and B and your own knowledge. (For guidance on answering this type of question, see pages 68–70.)*

Tasks

2. *Study Source C. Working in pairs, present a case to explain why the photograph should have been published.*

3. *Working in pairs, create two newspaper headlines and articles, one attacking and one defending the banning of the Daily Worker.*

The work of the Ministry of Information

In order to make sure that propaganda and censorship were carried out effectively, the Ministry of Information was set up within hours of the outbreak of war. By the end of the war, more than 3000 people worked in the ministry. At first the Ministry of Information was not very successful and some of its poster campaigns failed to win much support.

A poster has many purposes – to encourage, to sell, to convince, to appeal, to educate – but the first ones tended to alienate people. For example, Source D was felt to be divisive and not inclusive because it seemed to put the burden on the individual rather than the nation as a whole.

The Ministry of Information sought to tell the British people what they should do for the war effort, and this sometimes meant telling them what they could not do. Source E describes a range of campaigns and instructions given to people. There were also campaigns such as asking people to grow more food, to mend old clothes and not to discuss things openly in public.

As the war progressed some of the posters were extremely successful such as those used in the 'Dig for Victory' campaign, which encouraged everybody on the home front to become a vegetable gardener and grow more food (see Source F). The Ministry published huge numbers of pamphlets, books, short information films and newsreels to ensure that the morale of the population did not diminish.

Source D: One of the first posters of the Ministry of Information. It failed to win people over

YOUR COURAGE YOUR CHEERFULNESS YOUR RESOLUTION WILL BRING US VICTORY

Source E: From an interview with a member of the public by Mass Observation. (Mass Observation started in 1937 and looked at everyday life in Britain using untrained volunteer observers who kept diaries, answered questionnaires and interviewed members of the public)

In just one short walk I counted 48 official posters ... on hoardings, shelters, buildings, including ones to tell you to eat National Wholemeal Bread, not to waste food, to keep your children in the country, to know where the rest centre is, how to behave in an air raid shelter, to look out in the blackout, to look out for poison gas, to carry your gas mask always, to join the ATS, to fall in with the fire bomb fighters, to register for Civil Defence duties, to help build a plane, to recruit for the Air Training Corps, to save for Victory.

Source F: A 'Dig for Victory' poster

Source G: A poster encouraging people to cut down on the use of fuel

Tasks

4. *Suggest reasons why people disliked the poster in Source D.*

5. *What does Source E tell us about the effects of the work of the Ministry of Information?*

6. *How useful are Sources F and G as evidence of the work of the Ministry of Information? Explain your answer, using Sources F and G and your own knowledge. (For guidance on how to answer this type of question, see pages 68–70.)*

7. *Explain why Source G was a successful piece of propaganda.*

Radio

On 1 September 1939 the BBC closed down its television transmissions and they did not re-commence until 1946. (In 1939, there were about 20,000 television sets in Britain – all in London and the Home Counties.) However, the BBC continued to broadcast radio programmes to a huge audience. There were almost 9 million licence holders, which meant that almost every family had access to a radio. As a result it became a crucial method of involving the population and keeping them informed. The Ministry of Information had control of the BBC but it hardly ever interfered and the BBC became well versed in self-censorship.

The BBC newsreaders became very popular. At the outbreak of war it was decided that they should give their names at the start of each bulletin so that listeners would become accustomed to their voices and be able to detect a voice that was being impersonated by the enemy in the event of invasion.

BBC war reporters such as Richard Dimbleby and Frank Gillard sent back vivid accounts of British forces in action during the war and attracted huge audiences. (Dimbleby once recorded a report from a British bombing raid over Berlin for broadcast the following day.)

Radio programmes such as 'It's That Man Again' and 'Music while you work' became great favourites and maintained morale. 'It's That Man Again' was a comedy programme that poked fun not only at Hitler and the Germans but also at the British way of dealing with the war. 'Music while you work' was a programme introduced following a government suggestion that morale in industry would be improved if there were daily broadcasts of cheerful music piped into the factories. It proved to be most successful.

Source H: **A photograph of a family listening to the radio**

Cinema

Before the war the cinema was a cheap and therefore popular form of entertainment. In 1938, about 980 million cinema tickets were sold, and by 1945 this had reached more than 1500 million. The Ministry of Information produced many short films about coping with the problems created by the war and there were documentaries such as 'Fires were started' about fire fighting in London.

The British cinema industry also continued to make films during the war. The films were patriotic and dealt with the realities of war but obviously had a biased approach, such as 'In which we serve' and 'Went the day well?' One of the most famous films of the war was 'Henry V' starring Laurence Olivier. The film was made in 1943 and issued just before the D-Day invasion.

Task

8. *How useful are Sources H and I to someone studying Britain during the Second World War? Explain your answer, using Sources H and I and your own knowledge. (For guidance on answering this type of question, see pages 68–70.)*

Source I: A still from the film *Went the Day Well?* The film was made in 1942 and was about the capture of a British village by German paratroopers. The villagers and the Home Guard eventually defeat the Germans

What was the impact of the war on food supplies?

In 1938, Britain imported 55 million tonnes of food, which was almost three quarters of its total consumption. More than half of the meat consumed was imported and the majority of cheese, fruit, cereals and fats came from abroad. The government had been making plans since 1936 to combat food shortages in the event of war and gradually food rationing was brought in (see tables on page 67). The government's fears about attacks on British **merchant ships** proved right, and by Christmas of 1939 the Germans had sunk 96 ships. The situation worsened and in one month alone, March 1942, the Germans sank 275 British merchant ships. As the Battle of the Atlantic developed, food stocks dwindled and Britain had to take drastic steps to ensure that not only was there sufficient food for everyone but that everyone received a fair and equal amount.

Rationing

The first stage in the rationing process was National Registration Day, 29 September 1939, when every householder had to fill in a form giving details of the people who lived in their house. The government then collated this data and issued everyone with an identity card and ration book. These books contained coupons that had to be handed to or signed by a shopkeeper every time rationed goods were bought, so people could only buy the amount they were allowed.

Lord Woolton became the Minister of Food and he oversaw the introduction of the rationing programme which was combined with a nationwide propaganda campaign to ensure that people did not waste food and grew as much of their own food as was possible. The government knew that there was a danger of food prices rising quickly as certain foods became scarce, so by intervening with price controls and rationing, ordinary people were never in any danger of being unable to afford the necessities of life.

In 1941, the government introduced a points system for rationed goods (which were given a specific points value) and each month a person could spend the allowance of 20 points on those goods that were available. The 'Dig for Victory' campaign encouraged people to turn their lawns into vegetable gardens. Many people in towns began to keep hens, rabbits and even pigs to supplement their ration allowances. In 1939, there were just over 800,000 allotments in Britain and this figure had almost doubled by 1943.

Despite the hardships caused by rationing, the people of Britain were healthier than before the war – they had a more balanced diet, even if it was rather boring. Fewer mothers died in pregnancy than before the war because they were given milk and orange juice to improve their health. Young children were also healthier because they were also given milk and orange juice.

The black market

There was, nevertheless, an illegal trade (**black market**) in rationed goods and people with money would pay higher prices. The government tried to stop such trade and Parliament passed laws that were quite severe. Courts could impose fines of up to £500 and imprison the guilty for up to two years. The Ministry of Food employed about 900 inspectors to try to root out the black market.

Item	When rationing began
Petrol	September 1939
Bacon, butter and sugar	January 1940
Meat	March 1940
Tea and margarine	July 1940
Jam	March 1941
Cheese	May 1941
Clothing	June 1941
Eggs	June 1941
Coal	July 1941
Rice and dried fruit	January 1942
Tinned tomatoes, peas and soap	February 1942
Coal, gas and electricity	March 1942
Sweets and chocolate	July 1942

Rationing timeline. Rationing continued on many items until 1954

Item	Allowance
Milk	1.6 litres (3 pints)
Meat	340–450 grams (12–16 oz)
Eggs	1 fresh (or 1 packet of dried eggs every two months)
Cheese	84–112 grams (3–4 oz)
Bacon and ham	112 grams (4 oz)
Tea	56 grams (2 oz)
Sugar	224 grams (8 oz)
Butter	56 grams (2 oz)
Cooking fat	56 grams (2 oz)
Other rationed foods (usually tinned) subject to availability	20 points

An adult's weekly food ration allowance in 1943

Source C: From a textbook about Britain and the Second World War

Rationing was thought of as a necessary restriction during the war and people happily turned the queue into a national institution. Memories of wartime shortages during the First World War were associated with unfair distribution and profiteering. The Second World War was not to be like that. There were black markets, but the Ministry of Food was the biggest and fairest shop in the world.

Source B: A photograph of the Tower of London moat, published in 1940 with the caption 'Even the Tower of London moat was turned into a vegetable garden'

Tasks

1. *Study Source A. What can you learn from Source A about food problems by 1941? (Remember how to answer this type of question? For guidance, see page 12.)*

2. *Write a brief explanation of why rationing was introduced during the war.*

3. *Explain why Source B was published in many newspapers during 1940.*

4. *Explain why most people favoured rationing.*

5. *What does Source C mean by the phrase 'people happily turned the queue into a national institution'?*

Examination practice

This section provides guidance on how to answer the utility question from Unit 3, which is worth ten marks.

In answering the utility question, you must analyse various aspects of two sources and, in order to reach the top level, you need to cover them all. The content and the nature, origin and purpose (NOP) of a source should be considered and out of this there will emerge an evaluation of the source's utility and reliability.

In order to reach higher level marks for this question you have to explain the value (usefulness) and limitations of both the content and the NOP of each source. The NOP is found in the provenance of the source – the information given above it. A good tip is to highlight or underline key words in the provenance, which show either the utility or limitations of the source. An example of this approach is given in Source A on page 69.

There is also guidance in the box below about what to consider for the NOP of a source.

NOP means:

N Nature of the source.
What type of source is it? A speech, a photograph, a cartoon, a letter, an extract from a diary? How will the nature of the source affect its utility? For example, a private letter is often very useful because the person who wrote it generally gives their honest views.

O Origins of the source.
Who wrote or produced the source? Are their views worth knowing? Are they giving a one-sided view? When was it produced? It could be an eyewitness account. What are the advantages and disadvantages of eyewitness accounts?

P Purpose of the source.
For what reason was the source produced? For example, the purpose of adverts is to make you buy a product. People usually make speeches to get your support. How will this affect the utility of the source?

Question 1 – utility

How useful is Source A as evidence of attitudes towards rationing in the Second World War? Explain your answer, using Source A and your own knowledge.

How to answer

In the exam the question will be on two sources, but in question 1 we look at one source to help you build your skills in analysing a source. Question 2 on page 70 is about two sources. First let us concentrate on content. You should think about the following questions:

1. What is useful about the content of the source?

- What does it mention? How useful is this compared to your own knowledge of the event? This is known as your contextual knowledge.
- What view does it give about the feelings of people? Given your contextual knowledge, how typical is the view of the time?

For example:

> Source A gives the view that although there was rationing, some dissatisfaction was expressed by some people about the situation being unfair. This is interesting because the standard view is that people put up with it and were only disappointed with the boring nature of the food.

2. Are there any limitations to the content?

- Does it give a very limited or one-sided view?
- What does it not tell us about the event or person?

For example:

> Source A, on its own, is of limited use because it does not give us an idea of 'which sections' of people or where the information has come from.

Now let's move on to NOP. Below are examples of the values and limitations of the NOP of Source A as evidence of the attitude towards rationing.

Value

Nature. This suggests it is useful because it is from a report to the Ministry of Information and helps us understand the government's approach to rationing.

Origins. This makes it useful because it was published at the height of the war and when the last items of food were rationed.

Purpose. This is useful because it is an example of how policy was made during the war. In addition, the report helps us to understand that the government was keen to find out what people felt.

Limitations/Unreliability

Nature. This is of limited use because there is no notion of how widespread dissatisfaction was and it is not possible to know when any people were interviewed.

Origins. This makes it less reliable and useful because it was a report for the ministry whose job it was to support rationing.

Purpose. The report has given a clear picture of some views but the rich were only a minority and it seems that the report wanted to push rationing further so that the government would be seen to be making sure all people were involved in the 'sacrifice'.

Source A: From a **report** of the Home Intelligence department of the **Ministry of Information**, July 1942

There is growing evidence of a feeling among certain sections of the public that 'everything is not fair and equal and that therefore our sacrifices are not worthwhile.' In particular, there is some belief that the rich are less hit by rationing than 'ordinary people' for the following reasons:
a) They can eat at expensive restaurants.
b) They can afford to buy high-priced goods in short demand, such as salmon and game.
c) They can spend more on clothes and therefore use their coupons more advantageously.
d) They receive preferential treatment in shops, as 'people giving large orders' are favoured while poorer people wanting 'little bits' are refused.

Now have a go yourself

Answer question 1 using all the guidance given on these two pages. Make a copy of the planning grid on the right and use it to plan your answer. Include the value and limitations/unreliability of the contents of the source. If you need further guidance on this see page 87.

	Planning grid	
	Value	**Limitations/Unreliability**
Contents		
What does the source tell you?		
What view does the source tell you?		
NOP		
Nature		
Origin		
Purpose		

The utility of two sources

For Unit 3 you will need to evaluate the utility of two sources.

Question 2 – utility

How useful are Sources B and C as evidence of the impact of rationing in the Second World War? Explain your answer using Sources B and C and your own knowledge.

Source B: Eleanor Roosevelt, wife of US President Roosevelt, writing about her stay at Buckingham Palace in October 1942

The restrictions on heat and water were observed as carefully in the royal household as in any other home in England. There was a plainly marked black line in my bathtub above which I was not supposed to run the water. We were served on gold and silver plates, but our bread was the same kind of war bread every other family had to eat and except for the fact that occasionally game from one of the royal preserves appeared on the table, nothing was served in the way of food that was not served in any of the war canteens.

Source C: From *Don't You Know There's a War On?*, 1989. The book comprises the experiences of people who lived through the Second World War. This extract was written by a woman who had lived in Liverpool during the Second World War

There was quite a lot of black market going on – in eggs, butter, meat, bacon and that sort of thing – for those that could afford it. I don't blame them, if they had the money. Of course the rationing was a bit of a bug really, but on reflection it was good for us. They do say it was a very healthy time. I used to cook a lot of my own stuff. You only got meat once a week, and I used to use a lot of dried egg and spam. A lot of stuff came over from America and it was horrible. We used to have a lot of chips, but then potatoes were rationed, so you couldn't have a lot of that. But we didn't starve, and we used to improvise a lot, making pies and things, much more than you do now.

How to answer

- Explain the value and limitations/reliability of the contents of the first source.
- Explain the value and limitations/reliability of the NOP of the first source.
- Explain the value and limitations/reliability of the contents of the second source.
- Explain the value and limitations/reliability of the NOP of the second source.
- In your conclusion give a final judgement on the relative value of each source. For example, one source might provide one view of an event, the other source a different view.

Make a copy of the grid on page 69 to plan your answer for each source. Below is a writing frame to help you:

Source B is useful because (contents) it suggests ....

Moreover Source B is also useful because of (NOP) ....

Source B has limitations/is unreliable because (contents) ....

Source B is also of limited use/is unreliable because (NOP) ....

Source C is useful because (contents) it suggests ....

Moreover Source C is also useful because of (NOP) ....

Source C has limitations/is unreliable because (contents) ....

Source C is also of limited use/is unreliable because (NOP) ....

In conclusion Sources B and C are useful because they ....

8 The changing role of women

Source A: A government poster of 1941

WOMEN OF BRITAIN
COME INTO THE FACTORIES
ASK AT ANY EMPLOYMENT EXCHANGE FOR ADVICE AND FULL DETAILS

Source B: A statement issued by a government minister during a radio broadcast of May 1941

Today we are calling all women. Every woman in the country is needed to pull her weight to the utmost – to consider carefully where her services would help most and then let nothing stand in the way of giving such services. Like her, many women have made their sacrifices already and are doing their utmost to win the war. But to those thousands who have not yet come forward I would say here and now that every one of us is needed.

Tasks

1. *Study Source A. What is the message of this poster? How does the poster put across this message?*

2. *Study Source B and use your own knowledge. What is the purpose of this broadcast? Use details from the broadcast and your own knowledge to explain your answer. (Remember how to answer this type of question? For guidance, see page 20.)*

Women played an important part in the Second World War, particularly in their contribution to the armed forces, and their work in heavy industry, farm work and transport. This, however, made little difference to the status of women in society in the years that followed the war.

This chapter answers the following questions:

- What contribution did women make to the war effort?
- What effects did women's contribution to the war have on the position of women, 1945–51?

Examination skills
This chapter provides an opportunity to practise some of the question types from Unit 3.

What contribution did women make to the war effort?

At the beginning of the war in 1939 many women registered for voluntary work with organisations such as the **Women's Voluntary Service** (WVS), but others demanded part-time work in industry. The government's reaction was to ask women to stick to their existing jobs or stay at home.

The work of women was not properly organised by the government until April 1941, by which time there were labour shortages as more men were conscripted into the armed forces. All women were forced to register for work. In October of the same year, a report was published by the Ministry of Labour which showed that 2 million more workers were needed in the armed forces and **war industries**. In December 1941, conscription for war work of women aged 19 to 30 was introduced.

From then on, the number of women working steadily increased. By 1943, 17 million women aged between 14 and 64 were either in the forces or in essential war work. That included 90 per cent of single women and 80 per cent of married women with children over fourteen.

The women's armed forces

The women's armed services included the WRNS (Women's Royal Naval Services), the WAAF (Women's Auxiliary Air Force) and the ATS (Auxiliary Territorial Service). The WRNS was the most popular service followed by the WAAF. By 1944, there were 450,000 women in these services, with 212,000 in the ATS. The women did the routine office, driving and domestic duties which freed the men up to do combat duty.

Source A: A government propaganda poster encouraging women to work

JUST A GOOD AFTERNOON'S WORK!

PART-TIME JOBS NOW OPEN IN LOCAL WAR-FACTORIES

PART-TIME WAR WORKER

JUST A GOOD AFTERNOON'S WORK

Source B: A photograph of student officers of the WAAF undergoing a training course before being commissioned to various RAF stations around the country, November 1941

Despite not being involved in combat, women did hard and often dangerous jobs too. They worked as mechanics, welders, pilots, carpenters and even gunners on anti-aircraft guns – although they were not allowed to fire the guns. 335 women were killed in the ATS and another 300 wounded. In the navy they overhauled and serviced torpedoes and depth charges and repaired ships. As well as carrying out administrative tasks in the army, they also drove **convoys**, acted as **dispatch riders** and worked in **intelligence**. Many of the **code-breakers** at Bletchley Park were women. Bletchley Park is an estate in Buckinghamshire that was used as the government code-breaking headquarters during the Second World War.

As with their male counterparts, many women entered the voluntary services as well as doing a full- or part-time job. By 1943, there were 180,000 volunteers in **civil defence** and a further 47,000 in the fire services. 130,000 women volunteered as messengers and dispatch riders for the Post Office. Many other women worked in medical centres, first-aid posts, mobile canteens and rest centres.

Tasks

1. *Study Source A and use your own knowledge. What was the purpose of this poster? Use details from the poster and your own knowledge to explain your answer. (Remember how to answer this type of question? For guidance, see page 20.)*

2. *Source A was not very successful in encouraging women to work. Can you think of a reason why?*

3. *How reliable is Source B as evidence of the part women played in the armed forces?*

Heavy industry and transport

Women worked in all kinds of industries. In aircraft factories they worked a sixteen-hour day, seven days a week, without bank holidays. Many worked in **munitions**. Others worked as engineers, mechanics and lorry, train and bus drivers.

By 1943, women had proved how valuable they were in the war effort. They occupied 57 per cent of the jobs in factories, and, when they were in direct competition with men, often showed that they could do better. The Ministry of Information published details of women's achievements. A woman welder produced '30 feet [9 metres] more than a man on similar work'. A woman in a munitions factory produced 120 pieces of equipment a day, compared to 100 by her male colleagues.

However, pay and conditions were often poor. Many of the women working in factories faced a twelve-hour day in places that were a long way from home. To avoid the risk of bombing, the new munitions factories were often built in remote areas, so travel to the factories was often difficult. Women's pay was lower than it was for men: women usually received about 75 per cent of a man's wage, even if they were doing the same job. In engineering, women earned 43 shillings (£2.15) a week when they started, compared to a man's pay of 65 shillings and sixpence (£3.28).

Source C: From the personnel manager of a war factory, 1942

They had been told stories of nice clean factories with everything up to date and all modern amenities. I am genuinely sorry for these girls who highlight some of the facilities that should be provided for them. Our canteen is not so good. Lavatory accommodation will revolt these girls.

Source D: The memories of a female factory worker, describing her experiences in 1942

Working in factories is not fun. To be shut in for hours on end without even a window to see daylight was grim. The noise was terrific and at night when you shut your eyes to sleep all the noise would start again in your head. Night shifts were the worst. The work was very monotonous. I think boredom was our worst enemy.

Source E: A young woman describes her working day in a factory in 1943

The room was about 40 yards long by 20 broad [37 metres by 18 metres]. There are three benches of small machines and a few large drilling machines on the floor. Altogether there are about 40 women and about a dozen men. My machine is a drilling one, and I am given a heap of small brass plates to drill holes in. It is quite dark when we come out – which strikes one with a curious shock of surprise, for one feels not so much tired, rather as if one has missed the day altogether.

Source F: From the memoirs of Kay Ekevall, who worked in a shipbuilding yard during the Second World War

By the end of my time we had managed to get wages similar to those of the male workers. On the whole the men didn't seem to resent the women, and the skilled men were friendly and helpful to the female trainees. As it was an essential war industry ... I suppose they weren't afraid for their jobs.

Tasks

4. *Study Source C. What can you learn from Source C about working conditions for women? (Remember how to answer this type of question? For guidance, see page 12.)*

5. *Study Sources D, E and F. How far do these sources agree about the working conditions for women? Explain your answer, using the sources. (Remember how to answer this type of question? For guidance, see pages 45–46.)*

The Land Army

Around 80,000 women volunteered to work in the **Land Army** and became known as land girls. British farming had to produce as much food as possible to protect the country from starvation. Land girls had no choice where they worked and were often **billeted** in remote areas in very basic conditions. During the war an extra 11 million hectares of land were ploughed up for arable crops.

Farmers doubted that women could do the physically demanding work needed on farms. Many were convinced they would not be able to drive tractors, plough and shear sheep. They were proved wrong. Women proved themselves more than capable of coping with tough jobs and handled animals well. Land girls were often badly treated and the pay was poor. In 1944, they earned £2.40 a week – less than the female average wage of £3 – and half of that went on lodgings.

Source G: A poster encouraging women to join the Women's Land Army

'We could do with thousands more like you..'

JOIN THE WOMEN'S LAND ARMY

Apply to NEAREST W·L·A COUNTY OFFICE or to W·L·A HEADQUARTERS 6, CHESHAM STREET, LONDON S.W.1

Tasks

6. *Study Source G. How does the poster encourage women to join the Land Army?*

7. *How useful are Sources D and G as evidence of the work of women? Explain your answer, using Sources D and G and your own knowledge. (Remember how to answer this type of question? For guidance, see pages 68–70.)*

8. *How important was the part played by women in the areas below? Copy and complete the table, giving a brief explanation for each of your answers.*

	Decisive	Important	Quite important	Unimportant
Heavy industry				
Armed forces				
Land Army				

What effects did women's contribution to the war have on the position of women, 1945–51?

The war brought few benefits for the position of women in society.

Benefits

The war did bring some benefits to women. The varied and skilled jobs women did during the war gave many women more confidence and self-respect. They showed that they could do the same jobs as men and, in many cases, they could do them better. Many women enjoyed the freedom and independence the war gave them. These changes came too late for many women, but their daughters would benefit in the 1960s when the women's movement campaigned for better rights.

Source A: A table showing the percentage of women in paid work

	Single women	Married women	All women
1911	69	10	35
1921	68	9	34
1931	72	10	34
1951	73	22	35

The number of married women in paid work had increased by 1951. There was some change in attitudes towards married women working. In the 1950s some women did find work when their children were growing up.

No change

Most men were not enthusiastic supporters of the new, independent role of women, nor were many women. The media continued to portray women in their stereotyped domestic role.

Once the war ended most women willingly left their wartime jobs because they wanted to return to the home. A government survey of 1947 revealed that 58 per cent of women believed that married women should not go out to work. Many had delayed having children during the war and now decided that they wanted to start families.

Furthermore, women's career opportunities were not drastically improved by the war. For example, the new opportunities in areas such as metal manufacturing and engineering only lasted as long as the war. The shutting down of nurseries after the war meant the end of jobs for women who had young children. Moreover, women continued to make only slow progress in professions such as medicine and law. As late as 1961, only 15 per cent of doctors and 3 per cent of lawyers were women.

In 1946, the Equal Pay Commission, set up in 1944, found that the average male manual worker's wage was £5.70 a week, while that for a woman was £3. The Commission did not recommend any changes, suggesting that women did different jobs from men, so equal pay was not an issue. The male was still seen as the main breadwinner.

Source B: A woman remembers married life after the war

After a while we settled to some sort of married life but there were times when I thought it was hell on earth I was living in. Many of us felt as though we were going back to prison.

Tasks

1. *Make a copy of the scales and, using the evidence on this page, including Sources A and B, write in changes and lack of change.*

2. *Overall, did the war change the position of women? Use your evidence from task 1 to help you answer.*

D-Day and the defeat of Germany

Source A: From an interview with Private First Class James Jordan who was recalling his landing on Omaha Beach, 6 June 1944

The entire beach was a killing field. Artillery and machine gun fire were exploding all around me. Men were lying dead and wounded on the beach. Since I had lost my rifle along with my gear, I picked up one lying on the beach and began running forward with the aim of reaching a 3–4 foot [0.9–1.2 metres] high sea wall about 200 yards [183 metres] inland. I heard a shell pass over my head, I immediately hit the ground again. The shrapnel from the explosion passed over me but hit five men who had just reached the sea wall in front of me. Two of the men were killed instantly.

Task

Study Source A. What can you learn from Source A about the US landings on Omaha Beach on 6 June 1944? (Remember how to answer this type of question? For guidance, see page 12.)

By 1943, the Allies had started to have their own successes in the war. The Germans and Italians surrendered in North Africa in May 1943, and on the **Eastern Front** German forces suffered disastrous defeats at Stalingrad and Kursk. Stalin felt that the Soviet Union was bearing a disproportionate burden of the fighting and thought that his Allies were content to see his country permanently weakened. A second front was eventually established in June 1944, when the Normandy landings took place. After initial success with the landings, the Allies were slow to move out of Normandy but took Paris by August. Progress was slow in the autumn, when a daring operation launched to capture bridges over the Rhine failed. However, Hitler's last gamble at the Battle of the Bulge failed in January 1945, and thereafter it was only a matter of time before Allied forces in the West and East crushed Germany.

This chapter answers the following questions:

- Why did the Allies invade Normandy in 1944 and how did they prepare for it?
- What were the events of D-Day, 6 June 1944?
- What advances were made by the Allies in the West, 1944–45?
- What developments took place on the Eastern Front, 1943–45?
- What other reasons contributed to the defeat of Germany?

Examination skills

In this chapter you will be given further guidance on how to answer the reliability question, which is worth ten marks.

Why did the Allies invade Normandy in 1944 and how did they prepare for it?

Source A: A British cartoon of 1943. The cartoon shows Churchill altering the writing on the wall

SECOND FRONT at the right moment NOW

BASIC WINSTONESE

As soon as the USA entered the war in 1941, there were meetings between senior US and British military staff and politicians. In January 1943, US President Roosevelt and Winston Churchill met in Casablanca to decide on the future invasion of Europe. Here it was decided that as soon as the Germans and Italians were defeated in North Africa, there would be an invasion of Sicily. It was also agreed that the bomber offensive on Germany would be increased and the **USAAF** would assist the RAF in this campaign.

Decisions taken at Casablanca were confirmed at Tehran in December 1943, when Stalin, Roosevelt and Churchill met together for the first time. Stalin wanted pressure to be taken off the Eastern Front and the '**Big Three**' now agreed that a Second Front would be opened in May or June of 1944. Nevertheless, there was some tension between the leaders because Stalin continued to think that Churchill was not fully convinced about the Second Front.

After the conference, US General Dwight Eisenhower was made Supreme Commander of the Allied Expeditionary Forces. Plans were then drawn up for the invasion under the codename of 'Operation Overlord'.

Operation Fortitude

Initially, there was much debate about the actual site of the landings. There were three options – Brittany, Normandy and the *Pas de Calais*. Brittany was heavily defended, Normandy had no viable port and, for this reason, many senior commanders felt that the *Pas de Calais* was the best choice because it offered the shortest distance to the European mainland from Britain. It had good beaches on which to land military vehicles and was the direct overland route to Germany. However, it was the most heavily fortified and defended area along the Channel coast. Therefore, Normandy was selected for the site of the invasion. Once Normandy had been chosen, secrecy was paramount. Moreover, it was imperative that the Germans were convinced that the invasion would take place in an area other than Normandy. The whole deception plan was named Operation Fortitude.

The British had broken the German codes and, as a result, had knowledge of German troop movements and the positions of German army reserves. A double agent, codenamed Garbo, was used by the British to convince the Germans that the invasion would be a two-pronged thrust based on Normandy and Calais, with the more important attack coming at Calais. The deception plan kept German attention focused on the *Pas de Calais* and, as a result, the Germans based some of their best troops in that area.

Operation Fortitude also convinced the Germans that there was a First US Army Group stationed in south-east England. There was no such group. There was also a fictitious Fourth Army Group in Scotland that was ready to invade Norway. Fake army camps, vehicles and landing craft were also placed in the south-east of England to convince the Germans that the *Pas de Calais* was to be the scene of the invasion. As Operation Overlord developed, the actual day of the invasion became known as **D-Day**.

Overlord. Key items were landing craft (vessels to take soldiers and vehicles to the beaches) and also gliders. The gliders were to be used to land thousands of troops behind enemy lines before the assaults on the beaches took place.

Source B: **A photograph of an inflatable dummy Sherman tank in Kent, 1944**

Source C: **Higgins boats, which were manufactured in the USA and used as landing craft during the Normandy invasion**

Preparations for D-Day

The use of photographs

The Allies took countless aerial photographs of the Normandy area and the **French Resistance** provided information on German defences and troop deployments. Civilians in Britain were asked to send holiday postcards and photographs of the whole of France to the BBC, and the ones of Normandy were then used by the intelligence services in preparation for the invasion.

The influx of troops and materials

As hundreds of thousands of US soldiers came over to Britain there had to be meticulous planning. There were also thousands of other soldiers from Allied nations and training, feeding and keeping them occupied created logistical problems. There was more than a year of training for some of the troops and many were killed during manoeuvres.

The USA also sent over huge quantities of military materials in preparation for Operation

Tasks

1. *Study Source A and use your own knowledge. What was the purpose of this cartoon? Use details from the cartoon and your own knowledge to explain your answer. (Remember how to answer this type of question? For guidance, see page 20.)*

2. *How useful is Source B as evidence of Operation Fortitude?*

3. *How useful is Source C as evidence of the preparations for D-Day?*

4. *Can you suggest reasons why the BBC asked for postcards and photographs of France?*

Aerial superiority

Before the invasion, the Allies needed to have air superiority and in the six months before D-Day more than 2600 German fighter pilots were killed as a result of constant attacks on *Luftwaffe* bases and aerial combat. There were specific bombing raids on the German aircraft industry, and by the end of May the *Luftwaffe* was virtually powerless. On D-Day it flew hardly any **sorties** to challenge the invasion.

As D-Day approached, the air campaign began to focus on preventing the Germans' ability to move their reserves. French and Belgian railways were crippled, bridges were demolished in north-west France, and enemy airfields within a 210 kilometre radius of the landing beaches were put under heavy attack. The raids were supported by increased attacks by the French Resistance. However, an unfortunate result of the Allied bombing raids was the death of about 10,000 French civilians.

Supplying the Allied forces

Perhaps the most important issue for the Allies was neither the invasion nor deception plans, but the ability to supply thousands of troops once the landings had been made. Floating harbours, nicknamed **Mulberries**, were constructed and an underwater pipeline carrying oil, nicknamed PLUTO (pipeline under the ocean), was built to ensure rapid delivery of fuel. Without these the invasion would have stalled.

Tasks

5. *Construct a mind map to show how the Allies deceived Germany about the invasion.*

6. *Why was the bombing campaign on Northern France so important to the Allies?*

7. *As a class, discuss how the Allies could justify the bombing of Northern France when it was known that many French civilians would inevitably be killed.*

A photograph of Mulberry Harbour at Colleville sur Mer, September 1944

What were the events of D-Day, 6 June 1944?

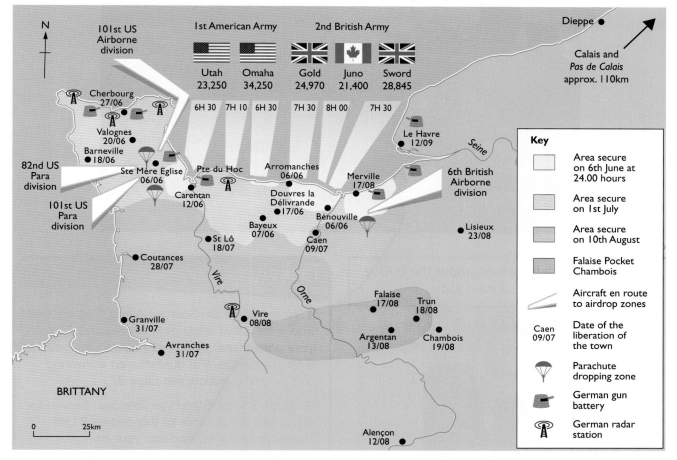

Map showing the deployment of Allied forces on D-Day and their movement inland during July and August

D-Day began on the night of 5–6 June 1944 when paratroopers and soldiers in gliders landed in Normandy. The US landed 15,500 airborne troops and the British 7900 behind enemy lines using almost 1000 gliders. Almost 7000 naval vessels assembled in the Channel off Normandy and the first landings at the designated beaches (Utah, Omaha, Gold, Juno and Sword) were made at 06.30 on 6 June. By the end of the day, the Allies had landed 156,000 troops with supporting mechanised vehicles. The Allied deception plans had worked. Even on D-Day, the Germans still continued to believe that the main attack would come at Calais and Hitler would not allow reserves to move to Normandy.

It has been estimated that Allied casualties on D-Day were about 10,000 including 2500 dead. The heaviest losses were sustained by the USA on Omaha Beach. By the end of July 1944, 1 million US, British, Canadian, French and Polish troops and hundreds of thousands of vehicles and supporting material had been landed in Normandy. However, despite considerable Allied superiority in men and material, the Germans kept the Allies bottled up in Normandy for almost two months.

Source B: A British cartoon about the D-Day invasion, published in June 1944

Source C: From a US army report written on D-Day, about the landings on Omaha Beach

*As the landing craft reached the beach the men faced heavy shelling, machine gun fire and rifle fire. It came from the **pill-boxes** and the cliffs above the beach. Men were hit as they came down the ramps of the landing craft and as they struggled through the defences towards the land. Many others were killed by mines. The enemy now started shelling the beaches which were full of US soldiers.*

Tasks

1. *How reliable are Sources A and C as evidence about the Allied landings in Normandy? Explain your answer using Sources A and C and your own knowledge. (For guidance on answering this type of question, see page 87.)*

2. *Study Source B and use your own knowledge. What was the purpose of this cartoon? Use details from the cartoon and your own knowledge to explain your answer. (Remember how to answer this type of question? For guidance, see page 20.)*

3. *Write an article for a British newspaper reporting about the Normandy landings.*

4. *Work in pairs. Look back at pages 78–81. Construct a mind map to show why the Allied landings were successful. Then number the reasons on your mind map in order of importance.*

What advances were made by the Allies in the West, 1944–45?

Despite the successful establishment of secure areas on D-Day, the Allies found it difficult to break out into Normandy and beyond. The Allies' position was improved on 27 June 1944 when the port of Cherbourg was taken (see map page 81). This meant that the Allies now had a deep water port and no longer had to rely on the Mulberries. However, a more easterly port was still needed to bring in the huge amount of supplies needed for the ever growing forces.

A major breakthrough came in August, at Falaise when much of the German Seventh Army and the Fifth *Panzer* Army were surrounded (see map page 81). In the space of just over a week, the Germans lost more than 10,000 dead and had 50,000 troops taken prisoner. When US President Eisenhower visited the scene two days after fighting ended, he said it was possible in places 'to walk for hundreds of yards at a time stepping on nothing but dead and decaying flesh'. After Falaise, the Allies advanced rapidly and on 25 August Paris was liberated. The Allies then moved towards Belgium and Luxembourg, but as the autumn approached, the advances slowed.

The Allies continued to face supply problems – Cherbourg was still the main port for bringing in material, as the Channel ports that were closest to England, such as Calais and Dieppe, were still in German hands (see map page 81). However, if the war could be brought to a quick end, the Allies' supply problems would be of little importance. In his desire to hasten the end of the war in the West, Field Marshal Montgomery suggested an airborne attack behind the German lines. This was codenamed Operation Market Garden.

The plan was to secure key Rhine bridges so the Allied forces could advance rapidly northwards and skirt around the German defences by wheeling into the lowlands of Germany. It was estimated that success would mean that the Western Allies would be in Berlin by Christmas 1944.

The operation began on 17 September 1944 when more than 30,000 British and US troops were flown behind enemy lines to capture the eight bridges on the Dutch–German border. There were successes at first but the key Rhine bridge at Arnhem was not taken, and the British First Airborne Division suffered heavy losses there. Logistical problems such as bad weather, poor radio communication and poor intelligence (which failed to detect the presence of the Second SS *Panzer* Corps) contributed to the failure. Following the failure at Arnhem, the forces were pulled back.

Source B: **From comments made by Montgomery after the failure of Operation Market Garden**

In my prejudiced view, if the operation had been properly backed from its inception, and given the aircraft, ground forces, and administrative resources necessary for the job, it would have succeeded in spite of my mistakes, or the adverse weather, or the presence of the Second SS Panzer Corps in the Arnhem area. I remain Market Garden's unrepentant advocate.

The Battle of the Bulge, December 1944–January 1945

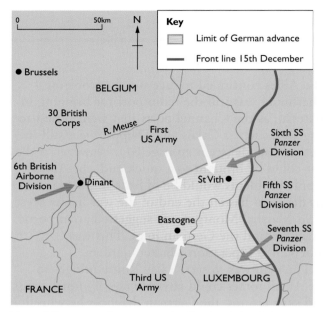

Map of German advances at the Battle of the Bulge

In December 1944, Hitler made his last attempt to defeat the Allies in the West. He wanted to split the Allied forces and prevent them from using the port of Antwerp, Holland. The Allies were still experiencing supply problems (it was taking 23 litres of fuel to deliver just 4.5 litres to the front). If successful, Hitler hoped that Britain and the USA would make a separate peace, independent of the Soviet Union. He was optimistic that Germany could develop new weapons (for example, jets, super tanks) which would help defeat Stalin.

The offensive was made through the Ardennes and achieved total surprise. The attack was planned in secrecy with almost total radio silence, and hundreds of tanks and vehicles were moved to the front without the Allies' knowledge. The attack was launched on 16 December 1944, when poor weather prevented any Allied flights. There was initial success for the Germans and they made rapid advances into Belgium and Luxembourg, creating a 'bulge' in the US lines (see map above). There was savage fighting around Bastogne, where US forces were surrounded but eventually German forces ground to a halt. They too suffered supply problems and by the end of January 1945, they withdrew to their defensive lines.

US casualties were about 80,000 and the Germans suffered about 100,000. However, the results of the Battle of the Bulge were devastating for the Germans. Their final reserves had been used and German forces found themselves being pushed back in the West and the East and they could no longer hold back the Allies' juggernaut.

In March 1945, the Allies pushed across the River Rhine and at the beginning of May, Soviet forces captured Berlin (see page 85). Hitler committed suicide on 30 April and the Germans surrendered unconditionally on 8 May.

Many historians have commented on how long it took the Allies to move from Normandy into Germany considering the advantages they possessed in terms of men and supplies. It has been suggested that the closer the Allies moved to Germany, the less willing soldiers were to risk their lives because they knew that the war would soon be over.

Tasks

1. *What does Source A (page 83) tell us about the Allied advance in France in August 1944?*

2. *What was the purpose of Operation Market Garden?*

3. *Study Source B (page 83). What can you learn about Operation Market Garden from Source B? (Remember how to answer this type of question? For guidance, see page 12.)*

4. *What is meant by the term 'Battle of the Bulge'?*

5. *Make a list of reasons why Hitler thought that Britain and the USA would make a separate peace, independent of the Soviet Union?*

What developments took place on the Eastern Front, 1943–45?

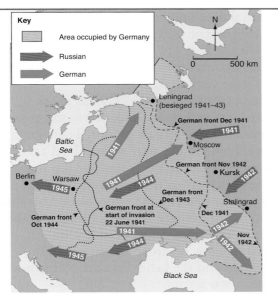

The Germans suffered two major defeats against the Soviet Union on the Eastern Front in 1943 – at Stalingrad in January and Kursk in July. By the summer of 1943, the Germans were outnumbered three to one in tanks and the Soviet Union was manufacturing them at an astonishing rate. A further Soviet Union victory came when the siege of Leningrad ended in January 1944. The attack on Leningrad had been the northern part of the German invasion of the Soviet Union and the city had been besieged for almost two and a half years.

What marked out the war in the East was the intensity, savagery and scale. Millions of soldiers and civilians were killed. The Germans killed civilians wantonly as they invaded the Soviet Union and as they retreated. No one knows the exact number of dead Soviet civilians, but the figure is between 7 and 20 million. The Germans considered the Soviet civilians as sub-humans (*Untermenschen*) and hence they were not accorded normal human treatment.

By the end of 1944, there were no German troops occupying the Soviet Union and after a lull

in the fighting the Soviet advance began again in mid-January 1945. By April 1945, Soviet forces had liberated Poland, Hungary and Austria. They took Berlin on 2 May following an assault by about 1.5 million soldiers. The Soviet Union had taken on the main part of the German army and had eliminated more than 600 German divisions (a division was about 12,000 men).

The surrender of Germany

The first Instrument of Surrender, the official document indicating the end of fighting, was signed at Rheims, France, at 02:41 hours on 7 May 1945. The German High Command issued orders to all forces under its command to cease active operations at exactly 23:01 hours on 8 May.

Source B: **From a book about the Soviet Union**

Stalin succeeded in galvanising the nation for total war. He appealed to Russia's traditional patriotism. The call was to fight for 'Mother Russia', a call with the widest appeal. The country was able to mobilise 16 per cent of the population for military service. The privations of war were shared out so that food distribution was maintained in most instances. It is probable that one in seven of the pre-war Soviet population – approaching 30 million – died during the war, a figure just under half of the total war casualties for all nations.

Tasks

1. *What can you learn from Source A about the Soviet advance into Eastern Europe in 1945?*

2. *What can you learn from Source B about the Soviet Union and the Second World War? (Remember how to answer this type of question? For guidance, see page 12.)*

What other reasons contributed to the defeat of Germany?

Source A: A table of military production of the combatants in the Second World War

Military production	Allies	Germany and allies
Tanks and self-propelled guns	227,235	52,345
Artillery	914,682	180,141
Machine guns	4,744,484	1,058,863
Military aircraft	633,072	278,795
Destroyers	814	86
Submarines	422	1,337

In addition to the advances on the Eastern and Western fronts, the following factors contributed to the eventual defeat of Germany:

- The Allies had access to tremendous industrial and military resources against which Germany and its allies found it impossible to compete.
- The invasion of the Soviet Union meant that Hitler had to fight a war on two fronts and, in addition, he had to send several divisions to assist Italy in North Africa and then in Italy itself.
- Allied bombing raids on Germany played their part in the defeat of Germany. The RAF and USAAF destroyed industrial complexes, roads, bridges, railway yards and munitions factories. However, the output of German industry did not decline until early 1945 and it is difficult to measure the impact of a bombing campaign on civilians. Nevertheless, Churchill could have looked at the impact of the Blitz and other German bombing campaigns on British civilians, where the spirit of the people was not broken and, if anything, the bombing made civilians more resolute in their desire to win the war.
- The war at sea was a failure for Germany. The **U-boat** threat was a major problem in 1942 when almost 1200 Allied ships were sunk. But technical developments – sonar, depth charges and centimetric radar – helped the Allies to combat the U-boats. The Allies were able to replace destroyed ships, and in 1944 only 117 ships were sunk by U-boats.
- German treatment of the civilians in the countries that they occupied led to the growth of resistance or **partisan group**s. These groups, especially in France, were given Allied assistance and meant that Germany had to keep many soldiers based away from the actual fighting.
- Historians often cite the errors caused by Hitler meddling in military affairs: for example, the halting of German tanks outside Dunkirk, his refusal to allow his troops to retreat from Stalingrad and the belief that the Normandy invasion was a feint.
- Hitler was faced with three powerful leaders, Churchill, Roosevelt and Stalin, who inspired their peoples throughout the war years.
- Ordinary people in Britain and the USA were united in the belief that they were fighting to rid Europe of tyranny. As a result, they felt that the sacrifices were worth enduring in order to forge a better future for the world.

Tasks

1. *What does Source A tell us about military production in the Second World War?*

2. *In groups, construct a rank order of the reasons for the defeat of Hitler. Give feedback to the class, explaining your rank order.*

Examination practice

This section provides guidance on how to answer the reliability question from Unit 3, which is worth ten marks.

Question 1 – reliability

How reliable are Sources A and B as evidence of the D-Day landings? Explain your answer using Sources A and B and your own knowledge.

How to answer

You are being asked whether you can trust what the source is suggesting.

- Compare what the source suggests to your own contextual knowledge. In other words, what you know about the person or event.
- Examine the nature, origins and purpose (NOP) of the source with reference to reliability. A reminder of what to consider for NOP is on page 68.
- Cross-reference the two sources to see if they support each other.

On the right is an example of how you could approach looking at the reliability of Source A.

Now have a go yourself

Analyse the reliability of Source B using the planning grid on the right. Then write an answer to question 1.

Nature. This is a photograph, which can only give one glimpse of the events and is not reliable in terms of the whole landings on D-Day.

Origins. This is reliable because it was taken on the day and the photographer was clearly witnessing the invasion and was an official photographer.

Purpose. This is less reliable because it is showing men walking on the beach landing quite easily. The photograph was to show how easy it all was.

Source A: An aerial photograph of US troops landing on Utah Beach, 6 June 1944. The photograph was taken by a USAAF photographer

Content. This is reliable because it shows US troops landing.

Contextual knowledge. This is reliable because US troops did land on Utah Beach and faced only a small amount of German opposition.

Cross-referencing. This is reliable because the image of the landings in Source A is supported by the comments made in Source B.

Source B: From a US reporter who witnessed the landings on D-Day

I was in a bomber above the landings for a few minutes. From what I could see there was nothing stopping the attacking soldiers from getting ashore. The Germans had been taken by surprise. There seemed little German resistance and soon wave after wave of Allied troops reached the shore almost unopposed. Everything seemed to go according to plan.

Source	Reliable	Unreliable
Contextual knowledge		
Nature		
Origins		
Purpose		
Cross-referencing		

Key Topic 4: Labour in power 1945–51

Source A: A cartoon published in the *Daily Mail*, 24 August 1948. The caption read 'Absolutely free – but you'd better get cracking before the supplies run out'

Task

Study Source A and use your own knowledge. What was the purpose of this cartoon? Use details from the cartoon and your own knowledge to explain your answer.
(Remember how to answer this type of question? For guidance, see page 20.)

This key topic examines the Labour government in power from 1945–51. It starts by looking at the reasons behind the Labour election victory in 1945 before going on to examine how the new government implemented the recommendations of the **Beveridge Report**, which attacked the '**Five Giants**'. It finishes by considering the establishment and operation of the National Health Service in 1948 and its impact in the years 1948–51.

Each chapter explains a key issue and examines important lines of enquiry as outlined below.

Chapter 10: Labour comes to power (pages 89–98)
- What were the key features of the 1945 general election campaign?
- Why did the Labour Party win the general election?

Chapter 11: Responding to the Beveridge Report: the attack on 'want' (pages 99–104)
- Why was the Beveridge Report drawn up?
- What were the recommendations of the Beveridge Report?

Chapter 12: The National Health Service (pages 105–111)
- What were the main provisions of the National Health Act, 1946?
- Why was there opposition to the act from the medical profession?
- What impact did the National Health Service have on the people of Britain in the years 1948–51?

10 Labour comes to power

Task

Study Source A. What can you learn from Source A about the expectations of British soldiers at the end of the war? (Remember how to answer this type of question? For guidance, see page 12.)

The war officially ended in Europe on 8 May 1945 and there were tremendous celebrations across the whole of Britain. Politicians began to think about a general election. On 21 May 1945, at the Labour Party conference, it was decided to reject Winston Churchill's suggestion that any election be postponed until the end of the war with Japan. Churchill formed a **caretaker administration** in preparation for the general election, which was set for 5 July. There had been a distinct move to the left in politics and many of the **coalition** government's wartime policies made people want a more socially just and fair society. A survey for the Ministry of Information in 1942 showed that people thought that things would be different and better after the war – after all, government **propaganda** had encouraged sacrifice with the prospect of a better future. What hardly anyone predicted was the victory of the Labour Party.

This chapter answers the following questions:

• What were the key features of the 1945 general election campaign?
• Why did the Labour Party win the general election?

Examination skills

In this chapter you will be given guidance on how to answer the hypothesis testing question, which is worth sixteen marks.

What were the key features of the 1945 general election campaign?

The general election in 1945 was the first to be held in Britain since 1935 and several million people were voting for the first time. The electorate was about 33 million and about 24 million people voted. The Labour Party had not held office since 1931 and political differences had created huge divisions within it during the **Depression**. It had recovered slowly during the 1930s but won only 154 seats in the 1935 election (the Conservatives won 432). There was still a fear of Labour's **socialist policies** and many people continued to raise the spectre of the creation of a **communist** state if Labour were ever to win a majority of seats. (Labour's two periods of office in 1924 and 1929–31 had been **minority governments**.)

In 1945, each of the two main parties published a **manifesto** indicating the policies they would follow if they were elected. Many of the policies were similar but Labour embraced the Beveridge Report (see Chapter 11) and said they would implement its recommendations immediately. The Conservatives were more careful about setting time limits.

The Conservatives had an aggressive election campaign that tried to smear the Labour Party but this turned out to be counter-productive. When the campaign began, it was anticipated that the Conservatives would win. Their main weapon was Churchill and he was well received wherever he went. However, in his first election broadcast (see Source D), he made a critical error of judgement, which many felt lost the Conservatives many votes. The broadcast became known as the 'Gestapo speech'. Some felt Churchill had misjudged the electorate because he was saying that Labour politicians such as Clement Attlee and Ernest Bevin – his colleagues in the coalition government – were no longer to be trusted.

Source A: Manifestos of the Labour and Conservative parties		
	Conservative Party	**Labour Party**
Manifesto title	*Mr Churchill's declaration of policy to the electors*	*Let us face the future*
Main policies	Comprehensive insurance scheme National Health Service Full employment Education improvements Housing improvements	Comprehensive insurance scheme National Health Service to be set up immediately Full employment Education improvements Housing improvements Nationalisation of the Bank of England, coal and power, transport, iron and steel to be carried out immediately. This policy would guarantee many jobs.
Comment	The Conservative manifesto emphasised the need for continuity under Churchill. Conservative posters also showed their reliance on Churchill. Though Churchill spoke of a clear plan, it seemed as if many policies were just hopes and not definite.	The Labour Manifesto stressed planning, reconstruction and equality – all policies that people had come to recognise during the war. Labour's campaign did not mention any personalities. The Labour manifesto showed that it would implement the Beveridge Report more quickly than the Conservatives. It put forward the idea of 'Never again' – a phrase that could be interpreted in several ways – not only referring to war but also to the poverty and unemployment of the 1930s.

HELP THEM FINISH **THEIR JOB!**
Give *them* homes and work!
VOTE LABOUR

The radio broadcasts for each party attracted huge audiences and the public meetings were extremely well attended. Public interest in politics and international events had grown during the war and the electorate was aware of the key issues facing Britain. Voting began on 5 July and ended on 19 July – this was to permit soldiers serving overseas to vote.

The election results were declared on 26 July 1945. Labour had won a landslide victory. Some of the Labour leaders had not expected this and had booked their summer holidays, which then had to be cancelled.

Source C: A Conservative Party campaign poster, 1945

CONFIRM YOUR CONFIDENCE IN CHURCHILL

PUT IT THERE !

Source E: A table of the 1945 general election results

Party	Seats	Percentage of seats in parliament	Percentage of votes cast	Percentage increase/ decrease on 1935 election
Labour	395	61.7	48.1	+10.4
Conservative and Ulster Unionist	215	33.6	40.1	-13.9
Liberals	12	1.9	9.0	+0.8
Others	18	3.4	2.8	

Tasks

1. *Study Source A. The policies of the two parties look very similar. What made the Labour Party more attractive to the voters?*

2. *How useful are Sources B and C as evidence of the campaigns of the Conservative and Labour parties in 1945? Explain your answer, using Sources B and C and your own knowledge. (Remember how to answer this type of question? For guidance, see pages 68–70.)*

3. *Study Source D. What was it that Churchill disliked about socialism?*

4. *Write a newspaper headline attacking Churchill's speech in Source D. (Avoid the use of the word 'Gestapo'.)*

5. *What can you learn from Source E about the general election result?*

Source D: From Winston Churchill's radio broadcast, 4 June 1945

No socialist government conducting the entire life and industry of the country could afford to allow free, sharp, or violently worded expressions of public discontent. They would have to fall back on some form of Gestapo, no doubt very humanely directed in the first instance … And this would nip opinion in the bud; it would stop criticism as it reared its head, and it would gather all the power to the supreme party and the party leaders, rising like stately pinnacles above their vast bureaucracies of civil servants, no longer servants and no longer civil.

Why did the Labour Party win the general election?

Wartime experiences

During the war, the Labour Party was fortunate to have some of its leading figures as key government ministers. Clement Attlee, the Labour leader, was Churchill's deputy and was frequently in charge of the country when Churchill was away attending important meetings. Ernest Bevin (Minister of Labour) and Herbert Morrison (Home Secretary and Minister for Home Security) held vital posts. These three men were crucial to the final victory and they became household names during the war. Furthermore, because the coalition government

Source A: A cartoon published in the *Daily Mirror* on Victory in Europe (VE) Day, 8 May 1945

"Here you are! Don't lose it again!"

followed 'war socialism' whereby the state controlled most industries and more importantly had a great say in the everyday life of its citizens, the fear that many people had about the socialist policies of the Labour Party now began to evaporate. There had been an acceptance of Labour's ideas and many people wanted them to be adopted after the war.

Evacuation

Evacuation (see pages 55–56) proved to be an eye-opener for many people. Not only were ordinary rural people surprised at the poverty of the urban children sent to live with them but many middle-class citizens were horrified at the condition of the evacuees. For example, over 12 per cent of evacuees from Newcastle-upon-Tyne did not have proper shoes and 50 per cent were infested with lice. Neville Chamberlain, the Prime Minister at the beginning of the war, said that he thought he knew all about the extent of poverty in Britain because he had been Minister of Housing for five years in the 1920s. He said evacuation showed that he did not know the true extent.

Housing

It was estimated in 1945 that about 1 million houses had been destroyed and damaged by the German bombing campaigns. Hence, both political parties said they would begin massive house building as soon as the election was over. The new modern homes would bring a new world and one that had been worth fighting for. J. B. Priestley, a left-wing writer and radio broadcaster, said that 'Britain was bombed into democracy'. Labour promised to build more houses than the Conservatives. In fact, Ernest Bevin, one of the leading Labour politicians, had promised to build 'five million homes in quick time'.

The Beveridge Report

The publication of the Beveridge Report in December 1942 (see Chapter 11) and the nationwide debate that followed convinced the British people, if not all politicians, that Britain would be a better place if its proposals were to be adopted. The Beveridge Report, with its attack on the 'Five Giants' (see Chapter 11), caught the mood of the nation and people wanted these giants to be attacked after the war.

US servicemen

The influence of the hundreds of thousands of servicemen from the USA must not be overlooked. The average height and weight of the US servicemen was greater than that of the average British soldier. The US soldiers were better paid. In addition, the US troops had access to many items that were denied to the average British soldier who had to endure rationing. What many British soldiers also noticed was the free and easy way officers and **GIs** got on in the US army – the opposite of the class-ridden structure of the British services. British soldiers were quick to ask why such differences existed.

Tasks

1. Personal research – find out about the work of Ernest Bevin and Herbert Morrison during the Second World War.

2. Explain why evacuation had such an impact on many people during the war.

3. What message is the cartoonist putting across in Source A?

4. Working in pairs, prepare a one-minute presentation to explain what J. B. Priestley meant when he said 'Britain was bombed into democracy'.

Interviewer: *Why do you think the nation turned against Churchill?*

Attlee: *Well, they didn't turn against him; they turned against the Tories. They remembered what happened in the thirties.*

Interviewer: *Was it also a matter of unemployment?*

Attlee: *I think the general feeling was that people wanted a new start. We were looking towards the future. The Tories were looking towards the past.*

Source D: **A BBC news broadcast, 26 July 1945**

Throughout the election campaign Mr Churchill had appealed to the country to give his new National Government a good majority. But the appeal was rejected by the people of Britain, largely, it is thought, because they believed Labour's promises to implement the Beveridge Report and its plans for creating a welfare state. At a news conference this evening, Mr Attlee promised a new world order and an economic policy to raise the standards of life for people all over the world. He said: 'We are facing a new era and I believe that the voting at this election has shown that the people of Britain are facing that new era with the same courage as they faced the long years of war.'

It is clear that the Conservative Party relied too much on Churchill. His popularity was never really questioned and it remained undiminished among the British people, but many voters were unwilling to trust the Conservative Party to run the country in peacetime. Unlike the Labour Party, the Conservatives did not produce many major figures (other than Churchill) during the war. Only R. A. Butler emerged and his lasting legacy was the 1944 Education Act (see pages 102–103).

People were ready for a change. The war had meant that everyone had had to make sacrifices and Labour's manifesto, the Beveridge Report (see Chapter 11) and a general feeling of optimism all contributed to the Conservatives' defeat.

However, it must be remembered that the British electoral system of **first-past-the-post** favoured Labour. The majority of the electorate did not vote Labour – they secured only eight per cent more of the vote than the Conservatives, yet won almost twice as many seats.

Source C: **From *Tides of Fortune* by Harold Macmillan, 1969. Macmillan was a leading Conservative during the 1945 election**

Vast crowds turned out in flocks to see and applaud Churchill. They wanted to thank him for what he had done for them. But this did not mean that they wanted to entrust him and his Tory colleagues with the conduct of their lives in the years that were to follow. They had been persuaded during the last years of the war, that immediately the struggle was over there would follow a kind of automatic Utopia. The British people would move with hardly an effort into a socialist or semi-socialist state under their own leaders, which would bring about unexampled prosperity in a world of universal peace. Nor had they forgotten or been allowed to forget the years before the war.

Tasks

5. *Study Source B. What can you learn from Source B about Clement Attlee? (Remember how to answer this type of question? For guidance, see page 12.)*

6. *Study Source C. What can you learn from Source C about the reasons for the defeat of the Conservative Party? (Remember how to answer this type of question? For guidance, see page 12.)*

7. *Study Sources B, C and D and use your own knowledge. How far do these sources agree about the defeat of the Conservative Party in 1945? Explain your answer, using the sources. (Remember how to answer this type of question? For guidance, see pages 37–38 and 45–46.)*

Tasks

8. *What message is the cartoonist putting over in Source E?*

9. *Re-read pages 92–95. Create a mind map of the reasons for the victory of the Labour Party in 1945. Place 'Labour victory' in the centre, like in the example on the right, and have the reasons radiating from the centre.*

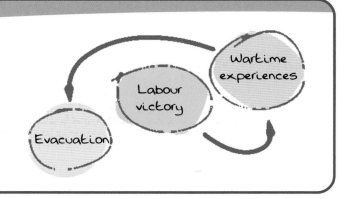

Examination practice

This section provides guidance on how to answer the hypothesis testing question from Unit 3, which is worth sixteen marks.

How to answer

In this question you are asked to use the sources to test a hypothesis – to decide which sources support and which sources challenge the hypothesis or view. At each level, you should make judgements on the reliability and sufficiency of the sources. Sufficiency means how much do the sources explain or show about the event or person. The examiner would expect you to write between one and two sides of A4.

Question 1 – hypothesis testing

'Winston Churchill was the main reason for the defeat of the Conservative Party in the 1945 general election.' How far do Sources A–F support this statement? Use details from the sources and your own knowledge to explain your answer.

Planning your answer

Make a copy of the grid below and complete it to help you plan your answer. Advice on how to write your answer is given on page 98. First study Sources A–F.

- Which sources agree with the interpretation?
- Why? Give a brief explanation in the grid. An example has been done for you.
- Which sources disagree with the interpretation?
- Why? Give a brief explanation in the grid. An example has been done for you.

Now briefly make a judgement on the reliability of each source. For further guidance, refer to page 87.

- In what ways is each source reliable? An example has been done for you.
- In what ways is each source unreliable? An example has been done for you.

	Agrees with interpretation	Disagrees with interpretation	Reliable	Unreliable
Source A	Churchill implies that people who vote Labour are no better than Nazis, implying those who want improvements are enemies of Britain.			
Source B		Suggests the class nature of the Conservative Party was a reason for failure.		
Source C				
Source D			Reflects the views of many people because they were some of the people represented on the roof.	Exaggerates Churchill's speeches to the people.
Source E				
Source F				

	Agrees with interpretation	Disagrees with interpretation
Own knowledge		

Source A: From Winston Churchill's election broadcast, 4 June 1945

No socialist government conducting the entire life and industry of the country could afford to allow free, sharp or violently worded expressions of public discontent. They would have to fall back on some form of Gestapo, no doubt very humanely directed in the first instance … Here in old England, we don't like to be regimented and ordered about and have every action of our lives prescribed for us.

Source B: From an election broadcast by Clement Attlee, leader of the Labour Party, June 1945

The Conservative Party remains as always a class party. In 23 years in the House of Commons, I cannot recall more than half a dozen from the ranks of the wage earners. It represents today, as in the past, the forces of property and privilege. The Labour Party is, in fact, the one party which most nearly reflects in its representation and composition all the main streams which flow into the great river of our national life.

Source C: From the autobiography of Herbert Morrison, written in 1960. Morrison was Home Secretary during the war and helped to write the Labour Party manifesto in 1945

The very honesty and simplicity of the campaign helped enormously. We had not been afraid to be frank about our plans. There would be public ownership of fuel and power, transport, the Bank of England, civil aviation, and iron and steel. We proposed a housing programme dealt with in relation to good town planning. We promised to put the 1944 Education Act into practical operation. We said that wealth would no longer be the passport to the best health treatment.

Source D: A cartoon published in the *London Evening Standard*, 30 June 1945. Churchill is addressing a crowd and he is flanked by people who are paid by the state

Source E: A cartoon from the *Daily Mirror*, June 1945. The man at the counter is saying 'What do you mean – you're out of stock – I've paid twice for these goods – once in 1914 and again in 1939!'

Source F: From a Labour Party election broadcast, June 1945

We are proud of the fact that our country in the hours of its greatest danger stood firm and united, setting an example to the world of how a great democratic people rose to the height of the occasion and saved democracy and liberty. We are proud of the self-sacrifice and devotion displayed by men and women in every walk of life in this great adventure. We call you to another great adventure which will demand the same high qualities as those shown in the war: the adventure of civilisation.

The diagram below gives you the steps you should take to write a good hypothesis testing answer. Use the steps and examples, along with your completed planning grid from page 96, to complete the answer to the question on page 96.

STEP 1
Write an introduction that identifies the key issues you need to cover in your answer and your main argument.

Example:
There is much debate over the reasons for the surprising Labour Party election victory of 1945. Some of the sources, most notably Sources A and D, suggest that it was due to the leadership of Winston Churchill. However, Sources B, C and F suggest it was due to the policies and approach of the Labour Party.

STEP 2
After your introduction, write a good length paragraph or paragraphs agreeing with the interpretation. Begin by identifying sources that support the hypothesis and then back this up with evidence from the sources themselves.

Example:
Sources A and D support the view that Churchill was responsible for the defeat of the Conservative Party. Source A, for example, is from a broadcast made by Churchill during the election campaign. The tone of the broadcast, especially the connection made between a Labour government and the Gestapo, did much to upset many voters.

Have a go yourself

Have a go yourself using evidence from the other sources that agree with the interpretation.

STEP 3
Make judgements on the reliability of the sources that agree with the interpretation.

Example:
Source D does suggest it was Churchill who contributed to the Conservatives' defeat because of his speeches. However, the cartoon is for a specific readership and presents an exaggerated view. It is unreliable as it is evidence of only one area in Britain (London) and could have been used to promote a dislike of Churchill.

Have a go yourself

Have a go yourself at evaluating the reliability of the other sources that agree with the interpretation.

STEP 4
Write a good length paragraph or paragraphs disagreeing with the interpretation. Begin by identifying the sources that challenge the hypothesis and then back this up with evidence from the sources themselves.

Example:
Sources B, C and F, however, challenge the hypothesis given in the question and suggest the result was due to the appeal and policies of the Labour Party. Source C clearly indicates what Labour intended to do and presents a wide range of social policies that attracted support.

Have a go yourself

Have a go yourself using evidence from the other sources that disagree with the interpretation.

STEP 5
Make judgements on the reliability of the sources that disagree with the interpretation.

Example:
Source C provides reliable evidence of the policies of the Labour Party. It was written by a senior Labour leader, well after the victory, but Morrison was the man who helped write the Labour manifesto. He had been a minister in the wartime coalition and knew what policies people would vote for - as he clearly explains.

Have a go yourself

Have a go yourself at evaluating the reliability of the other sources that disagree with the interpretation.

STEP 6
Write a conclusion giving your final judgement on the interpretation. Does the weight of evidence from the sources support or challenge the hypothesis? Explain your final judgement.

Example:
The weight of evidence suggests that the defeat of the Conservative Party was not primarily due to the leadership of Churchill. Only two of the sources support this view. Source D attributes some of the blame to the Conservative Party itself whilst Sources B, C and F place much more emphasis on the policies and appeal of the Labour Party and its leaders.

11 Responding to the Beveridge Report: the attack on 'want'

Source A: A cartoon published in a British newspaper two days after the publication of the Beveridge Report, 3 December 1942

> **Task**
>
> *What can you learn from Source A about the Beveridge Report?*

The British government was keen to call the Second World War a 'people's war' in order to give a sense of involvement. In June 1941, a committee was set up to look into the existing provision for **health insurance**. There was nothing revolutionary in this and nothing out of the ordinary was expected. However, as the work of the committee progressed it began to broaden its scope and its chairman, William Beveridge, looked at all aspects of problems which faced ordinary people in their lives. He called these problems the 'Five Giants'. The findings of his report eventually formed the framework of the 'welfare state' set up by the newly elected Labour government after 1945.

This chapter answers the following questions:

• Why was the Beveridge Report drawn up?
• What were the recommendations of the Beveridge Report?

Examination skills
In this chapter you will be given the opportunity to practise some of the question types from Unit 3.

Why was the Beveridge Report drawn up?

The government portrayed the war as a People's War and therefore there had to be some clear benefits for the sacrifices that were being made. Many people hoped that, in the future, the government would reform social security in order to cover more of the population. There were hopes that the healthcare system, where large numbers had to pay for treatment and frequently did not have funds to do so, would also be improved. In 1940, free milk was introduced for all children and hospital treatment was reformed (it was unrealistic to expect people to pay for treatment if their houses had been bombed).

The government also wanted to think ahead and plan for the future after the war. Therefore, in June 1941, Arthur Greenwood, a Labour cabinet minister, set up a committee to look into the provision of health insurance in Britain. Greenwood appointed William Beveridge as chairman and asked him to look into all existing **social insurance schemes** (those run by the state, private insurance companies and employers' schemes). Though the government provided for many of its citizens, there was a range of public and private schemes. Greenwood expected Beveridge to simplify the systems.

Almost as soon as Beveridge started his work, he began to move beyond what he had been asked to do, by looking at all aspects of social problems. Moreover, Beveridge recognised that what he and his committee saw for the future was already happening, namely, greater government involvement in the lives of ordinary people to ensure a secure existence. The issue for Beveridge was to persuade politicians to accept increased peacetime government involvement.

The report, entitled 'Social Insurance and Allied Services', was published on 1 December 1942 and within weeks it had sold 635,000 copies. Within two weeks of its publication, a public opinion poll said that nineteen out of twenty people had heard of the report and that nine out of ten wanted its proposals to be carried out. The British press, with the exception of the *Daily Telegraph,* welcomed the report.

In 1939:
• 21 million people were eligible for old age pensions
• 15.5 million were covered by government unemployment insurance
• 20 million were covered by national health insurance (no more than half of the population)

> **Source A: An extract from the Beveridge Report showing the three guiding principles of the proposals that were put forward**
>
> *1) The proposals should not be restricted by consideration of **sectional interests**.*
>
> *2) The organisation of social insurance should be treated as part of a comprehensive policy of social progress. Social insurance may provide income security; it is an attack on want. But want is only one of Five Giants on the road of reconstruction and in some ways the easiest to attack. The others are disease, ignorance, squalor and idleness.*
>
> *3) Social security must be achieved by co-operation between the state and the individual. The state should offer security for service and contribution. The state should not stifle incentive, opportunity, responsibility – in establishing a national minimum, it should leave room and encouragement for voluntary action by each individual to provide more than that minimum for himself and his family.*

Source B: A cartoon of December 1942, shortly after the publication of the Beveridge Report. The face on the jug in the soldier's hand represents William Beveridge, the author of the report

SOCIAL SECURITY

Here's to the brave new world!

Source C: From the *Picture Post*, February 1943. The *Picture Post* was a popular magazine that sold about 1 million copies per week during the war

Parliament recognized the justice of the report. They could not make promises for the future. Sir Arnold Gridley wondered 'how want is to be defined. Can it necessarily be met by any specific monetary sum? The family of a hard-working and thrifty man can live without want, perhaps on £3 a week, whereas the family of a man who misuses his money or spends it on drink or gambling, may be very hard put to it if his wages are £5 or £6 a week.' The fear that small children or old age pensioners may take to drink or gambling is a very real one to large sections of the Conservative Party.

Tasks

1. Can you suggest reasons why the government portrayed the war as a People's War?

2. Explain why the Beveridge Committee was set up.

3. What did Beveridge mean when he said 'proposals should not be restricted by consideration of sectional interests'?

4. Study Source A. Working in groups, construct flow diagrams to show how the 'Five Giants' are linked.

5. Study Source A. Why was Beveridge keen to say that 'the state should not stifle incentive, opportunity'?

6. How reliable is Source B as evidence of the Beveridge Report?

7. Study Source C. What can you learn from Source C about the fears some people had about the Beveridge Report? (Remember how to answer this type of question? For guidance, see page 12.)

What were the recommendations of the Beveridge Report?

The report recommended a compulsory insurance scheme to eliminate poverty, whereby every worker would make contributions and these would be supplemented by contributions from employers and also the government. These contributions would help to build up a fund that would pay out weekly benefits to those who were sick or unemployed or who suffered industrial injury. In addition, the scheme would pay old age pensions. The scheme would support the worker and enable him and his family to survive in times of hardship. There would also be benefits for widows.

The report also proposed:

• a family allowance for the second child and subsequent children
• a marriage grant
• a maternity grant and benefit
• a death grant.

The key feature was that people were eligible to receive these benefits and grants because they had all contributed. Most importantly, the proposed system would end the hated Means Test of the 1930s (see pages 14–15).

The report's recommendations meant that the individual would be looked after by the state from the 'cradle to the grave' (others sarcastically said 'womb to the tomb'). If adopted, the report would create a 'welfare state'.

Beveridge argued that if his report were introduced, it would provide a minimum standard of living 'below which no one should be allowed to fall'.

Attacking the Five Giants

There were some reforms before the end of the war. Most important was the 1944 Education Act, which now ensured free education during the compulsory years. Parliament also passed the Family Allowances Act in April 1945, although the first payments were not made until August 1946. The key reforms came after the Labour government took office in July 1945 and attacked the Five Giants head on. In a period of just over three years the social reforms of the Labour government created a welfare state which attempted to look after all citizens whether rich or poor.

Tasks

1. *Study Source A. What can you learn from Source A about the Beveridge Report? (Remember how to answer this type of question? For guidance, see page 12.)*

2. *Explain what the phrase 'from the cradle to the grave' means.*

3. *Study the 1944 Education Act, 1945 Family Allowances Act and 1946 National Insurance Act. Give three reasons to explain the importance of each act.*

Ignorance

1944 Education Act
- Ministry of Education created
- Education divided into primary, secondary and further
- Secondary education to be divided into grammar, technical and modern, following assessment at 11
- Free education until school leaving age of 14 (raised to 15 in 1947)

Want

1945 Family Allowances Act
- 5 shillings (25p) per week for each child after the first one
- Allowance payable to the mother
- Payable until the child was 15 or 16 if the child was in full-time education

1946 National Insurance Act
- Ministry of National Insurance set up
- Unemployment benefit
- Sickness benefit
- Maternity benefit – single payment made to a mother on birth of a child
- Death grant to cover the costs of a funeral
- Widows' benefit
- Orphans – guardians to receive an allowance
- Old age pensions – men over 65 and women over 60 – single person 25s (£1.25p) and married couple 42s (£2.10) per week

1948 National Assistance Act
- Designed to help those 'who slipped through the net' of the new system
- Abolished the **Poor Law** system
- Chronic sick and those whose benefits were not enough were able to use the National Assistance Board (the National Assistance Board was created to assist people whose resources were inadequate)
- Homeless, disabled and mentally ill were covered by the act

Squalor

1946 Housing Production Executive set up
- One million houses built in the years 1945–51
- Thousands of pre-fabricated houses (prefabs) constructed

1946 New Towns Act
- 17 in England, 5 in Scotland, 1 in Wales. Peterborough, Crawley, Northampton and Warrington were enlarged

Attacking the Five Giants

Disease

1946 National Health Service Act (to come into operation 1948)
- Comprehensive service, with all citizens receiving all the advice, treatment and care they needed, combined with the best medical and other facilities available
- Service free to the public at the point of use

See Chapter 12 for further details

Idleness

- The wartime coalition had accepted that in peacetime it was the duty of government to maintain a high and stable level of employment. Labour, with its nationalisation of several industries, showed that it intended to manage the economy and fulfil the wartime hope. Moreover, building schemes ensured high employment for several years after the end of hostilities.

In the 'attack on want', the Labour government introduced the National Insurance Act. By this, all workers would pay a weekly contribution (4s 11d) and the employer and government would also contribute to the fund. The fund would then be used to pay benefits during periods of sickness or unemployment (see diagram on page 103). The act was hailed by all parties and the general public because it eliminated many of the injustices of the pre-war system.

To ensure that there would be no gaps in the welfare system and that there would be a guaranteed basic minimum income to everyone, the National Assistance Act was passed in 1948. A new National Assistance Board was set up to give benefits to those in need. By the act, all local authorities had to provide residential accommodation for the aged and handicapped and ensure that there was at least temporary accommodation for the homeless. *The Times* said that 'the National Assistance Board was the citizen's last defence against destitution'.

Source B: A photograph of a mother and her five children collecting her first family allowance, London, 6 August 1946

Source C: From *People in Change*, by J. Brooman, 1994

With 25 million workers in Britain in 1946, the National Insurance scheme was on a gigantic scale. The Ministry of National Insurance, which ran the scheme, had 40,000 staff in newly built offices in Newcastle. The records of insured workers were kept on 25 million sheets stored in 100 rooms. Throughout the country 992 local offices handled claims for benefits and passed them on to the headquarters in Newcastle.

Source D: From *Britain Since 1945*, P. J. Madgwick, 1982

Under the new Labour legislation, it was intended that the citizen would be adequately safeguarded against old age, sickness and unemployment, by an insurance-based system without the much resented Means Test. Poverty was not abolished, but the number of people seriously lacking in food, clothing, shelter and warmth was very substantially reduced compared with the 1930s.

Source E: From an interview in 1989 with a Ministry of Insurance official who had worked there in the 1940s

In 1948, it was an idealistic set-up. The central feeling was one of 'we are creating Jerusalem'. It was epitomised by the minister of National Insurance, who saw himself as being Father Christmas to the post-war generation.

Tasks

4. *Study Source B and use your own knowledge. What was the purpose of publishing this photograph? Use details from the photograph and your own knowledge to explain your answer. (Remember how to answer this type of question? For guidance, see page 20.)*

5. *What can you learn from Source C about the National Insurance scheme? (Remember how to answer this type of question? For guidance, see page 12.)*

6. *What can you learn from Source D about the effects of the National Insurance scheme? (Remember how to answer this type of question? For guidance, see page 12.)*

7. *Study Source E. What did the interviewee mean by the following phrases?*
'it was an idealistic set-up'
'saw himself as being Father Christmas'

8. *Draw a timeline for a man and a woman indicating the benefits they might receive from the welfare state from birth until death.*

12 The National Health Service

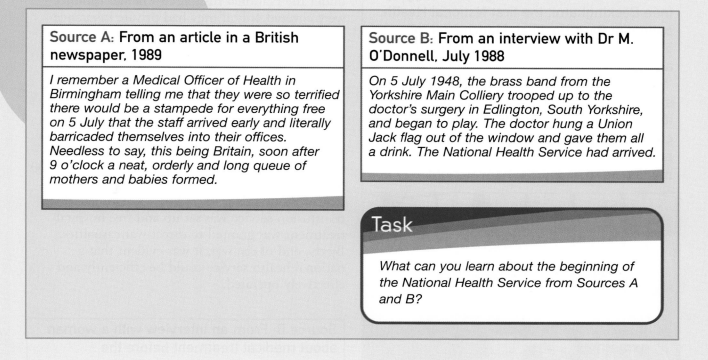

Source A: From an article in a British newspaper, 1989

I remember a Medical Officer of Health in Birmingham telling me that they were so terrified there would be a stampede for everything free on 5 July that the staff arrived early and literally barricaded themselves into their offices. Needless to say, this being Britain, soon after 9 o'clock a neat, orderly and long queue of mothers and babies formed.

Source B: From an interview with Dr M. O'Donnell, July 1988

On 5 July 1948, the brass band from the Yorkshire Main Colliery trooped up to the doctor's surgery in Edlington, South Yorkshire, and began to play. The doctor hung a Union Jack flag out of the window and gave them all a drink. The National Health Service had arrived.

Task

What can you learn about the beginning of the National Health Service from Sources A and B?

The introduction of the NHS was delayed because of opposition of the **British Medical Association** (BMA) but on 'the appointed day' (5 July 1948), there was great enthusiasm and anticipation in Britain. However, there had been no real analysis of immediate and future costs and within three years some charges were levied in dental and optical treatment. Charges for prescriptions were also eventually introduced. The man responsible for the introduction of the NHS was Aneurin Bevan, a staunch socialist. He resigned from the government in 1951, when charges were introduced.

This chapter answers the following questions:

- What were the main provisions of the National Health Act, 1946?
- Why was there opposition to the act from the medical profession?
- What impact did the National Health Service have on the people of Britain in the years 1948–51?

Examination skills
In this chapter you will be given the opportunity to practise some of the question types from Unit 3.

What were the main provisions of the National Health Act, 1946?

Source A: A photograph of Aneurin Bevan, Minister for Health, meeting Sylvia Diggory (née Beckingham), the first National Health patient at Park Hospital, Manchester, on 5 July 1948, the day the NHS began. In an interview 50 years later, Sylvia said: 'Mr Bevan asked me if I understood the significance of the occasion and told me that it was a milestone in history – the most civilised step any country had ever taken, and a day I would remember for the rest of my life – and of course, he was right'

In 1945, about half the population – the wage earners – were covered for free medical treatment under the National Insurance scheme. Families were covered only if they had private insurance and many of them did not have enough money to purchase insurance. Calling out a doctor, or going to a hospital, was often a last resort with the result that illnesses or injuries went untreated altogether, or became more serious than they might have been.

During the war, an Emergency Medical Service had come into operation and after the first four months of war the government had provided 1000 new operating theatres, millions of bandages and tens of thousands of extra beds. A national blood transfusion service was set up and free hospital treatment was granted to direct war casualties. By the end of the war, it was evident that a national health service could be efficiently and effectively operated.

Source B: From an interview with a woman about medical treatment before the introduction of the National Health Service. It was published in a book about the NHS in 1988

I was married in 1937 and if we ever needed to see the doctor, the fee was £1.05. We had to be really ill to consider facing up to this. The men did if they were not well enough to go to work, but the women very rarely bothered. My weekly household money was £1 and my husband's take home pay was £3. When my son was born in 1946, the hospital bill was £22 and the ambulance cost £1.25.

Task

1. How useful is Source A as evidence of the National Health Service?

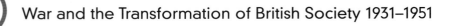

The Beveridge Report had anticipated a national service and the National Health Act was passed in 1946. Aneurin Bevan, was the leading figure in the development of the NHS but he met stiff resistance from the medical profession, which was worried about professional independence, potential costs and loss of status.

Source C: Aneurin Bevan speaking in the House of Commons, April 1946

A person ought not to be deterred from seeking medical assistance at the earliest possible stage because of the financial anxiety of doctor's bills. Our hospital organisation has grown up with no plan; it is unevenly distributed over the country.

In the older industrial districts of Britain hospital facilities are inadequate. Furthermore, I believe it is repugnant to a civilised community for hospitals to have to rely on private charity. I have always felt a shudder of repulsion when I see nurses and sisters who ought to be at their work, going about streets collecting money for the hospitals.

National Health Act, 1946

- The service was free to the public at the point of use.
- The service was comprehensive, with all citizens receiving all the advice, treatment and care they needed, combined with the best medical and other facilities available.
- Drug prescriptions, dental and optical care were included.
- Voluntary and local hospitals were co-ordinated into a single national system to be operated at local level by appointed Health Boards. The act took into national public ownership the 1771 English and Welsh local authority hospitals and the 1334 voluntary hospitals.
- The overall administration of the system was the responsibility of the Minister of Health.
- The NHS would control hospital and specialist services, general practitioner (medical, dental, ophthalmic and pharmaceutical) services, ambulance services and community health services.

Biography Aneurin 'Nye' Bevan 1897–1960

1897 Born in Tredegar, South Wales, one of ten children
1910 Left school and became a miner
1919 Won a scholarship to Central Labour College
1926 Leader of miners in Tredegar during the General Strike
1929 MP for Ebbw Vale
1945–51 Minister of Health
1951 Minister of Labour
1951 Resigned over NHS charges
1959 Elected Deputy Leader of the Labour Party

Tasks

2. *How reliable are Sources B and C as evidence of Britain's health service before a national system was introduced? Explain your answer, using Sources B and C and your own knowledge. (Remember how to answer this type of question? For guidance, see page 87.)*

3. *What were the results of the formation of the Emergency Medical Service?*

4. *Design two newspaper headlines, one praising and the other attacking the birth of the National Health Service.*

Why was there opposition to the act from the medical profession?

Source A: A cartoon published for the British Medical Association in 1946 after the passing of the National Health Act. Three doctors are saluting the emperor (Aneurin Bevan). Translated, the words at the foot of the cartoon say 'Those who are about to die salute you'

MORITURI TE SALUTANT.

The British Medical Association (BMA), the doctors' professional body, opposed the introduction of the NHS. Its members believed that they would lose money as a result of the NHS because they feared there would be no private patients. Their opposition to government interference went back to the beginning of the National Insurance scheme in 1911. The BMA had no wish for its members to become merely government workers and they fought to retain their independence. They did not wish to become salaried employees of the government – they said they would just be civil servants.

Source B: Alfred Cox, former Chairman of BMA, speaking about the National Health Service Bill, 1946

I have examined the bill and it looks to me uncommonly like the first step, and a big one, to National Socialism as practised in Germany. The medical service there was early put under the dictatorship of a 'medical führer'. This bill will establish the Minister for Health in that capacity.

In January 1948 the BMA held a ballot of all its doctors to see whether they approved of joining the NHS. Eighty four per cent of doctors voted and the result was 40,814 against and 4735 for joining. Despite this, Bevan specified that the new system would come into operation on 5 July of that year. Nevertheless, further talks followed and Bevan allowed the consultants to work inside the health service and at the same time still treat private patients and earn high fees. Bevan promised to amend the act accordingly and ended fears that doctors would become salaried civil servants. Following another vote among its members, the BMA recommended that its members participate in the new system. Bevan said he had ensured the start of the service by 'stuffing the consultants' mouths with gold'.

Source D: An extract from an article in *The Daily Sketch*, a British tabloid newspaper, February 1948, during the discussions between Bevan and the BMA

The state medical service is part of the socialist plot to convert Great Britain into a National Socialist economy. The doctors' stand is the first effective revolt of the professional classes against socialist tyranny. There is nothing that Bevan or any other socialist can do about it except in the shape of Hitlerian coercion.

Tasks

1. *Study Sources A, B and D. In what ways do the sources show that there was opposition to the introduction of the NHS?*

2. *What does Source C tell us about the introduction of the National Health Service?*

What impact did the National Health Service have on the people of Britain in the years 1948–51?

Source B: From an interview with Alice Law in 1984. She was recalling her mother's use of the newly established NHS in 1948

She went to the opticians. Obviously she'd got the prescription from the doctor. She went and got tested for new glasses. Then she went further down the road to the chiropodist. She had her feet done. Then she went back to the doctor's because she had been having trouble with her ears and the doctor said he would fix her up with a hearing aid.

By 5 July 1948, three-quarters of the population had signed up with doctors under the new health scheme. Two months later, 39,500,000 people, or 93 per cent of the population, were enrolled and more than 20,000 general practitioners, about 90 per cent, were participating. The new service had become immediately popular with the vast majority of Britain's population.

However, the government soon encountered problems with funding the system. In its first year the NHS cost £248 million to run, almost £140 million more than had been originally estimated. Annual sums put aside for treatment such as dental surgery and glasses were quickly used up. Initially, £2 million was put aside to pay for free spectacles over the first nine months of the NHS but this was spent within weeks. More than 5 million people were issued with NHS spectacles in the first year and millions visited the dentist in order to have all their teeth extracted and replaced with false ones. The Ministry of Health assumed that around 140 million free prescriptions would be

Source C: A cartoon published in the *Daily Express*, 22 December 1949

"Dentist says if there are any more of you thinking of fitting one another up with National Health teeth for Christmas presents you've had it."

Daily Express, Dec. 22nd, 1949

dispensed annually but this turned out to be a gross underestimate. The number of prescriptions increased each year until it reached 229 million in 1951. People even began to ask for free supplies of household remedies for which they had previously paid, such as aspirin, laxatives, first-aid dressings and cotton wool.

The government had estimated that the NHS would cost £140 million a year by 1950. However, by the beginning of 1949, costs were more than double this, reaching around £400 million and, by the time Labour left office in 1951, annual costs were almost £500 million. In 1951, the Labour government introduced a charge for some dental treatment and for prescriptions for medicine. This led to the resignation of Bevan.

When the Conservatives won the general election in 1951, they said they would retain the NHS, having firmly opposed the bill in 1946 and its establishment in 1948. The popularity of the NHS meant that no party now dared to threaten to dismantle it.

Source E: From *The Five Giants: A Biography of the Welfare State* by N. Timmins, 1995

In February 1950, Labour returned to power and the hunt for economy in the NHS resumed. In June 1950 the Korean War began and the defence budget again squeezed social spending. Gaitskell, the Chancellor, was adamant that charges for dental treatment and spectacles would be introduced.

Source F: From Aneurin Bevan's letter of resignation to Clement Attlee, April 1951, following the increasing costs of the NHS

It is wrong to impose national health charges because it is the beginning of the destruction of those social services in which Labour has taken a special pride and which were giving Britain the moral leadership of the world.

Source D: A cartoon published in the *Daily Express*, 21 September 1951. The date of the general election had just been announced. The caption read 'Watch out if them Tories get in – they'll want all yer teeth, glasses, 'air and bottles of free jollop 'anded back'

"Watch out if them Tories get in—they'll want all yer teeth, glasses, 'air and bottles of free jollop 'anded back."

Daily Express, Sept. 21st, 1951

Tasks

3. *Study Source D and use your own knowledge. Why was this cartoon published? Use details from the cartoon and your own knowledge to explain your answer. (Remember how to answer this type of question? For guidance, see page 20.)*

4. *Study Source F. What can you learn from Source F about Aneurin Bevan? (Remember how to answer this type of question? For guidance, see page 12.)*

5. *Study Source B (page 106) and Sources A, B, C, D and E (pages 110–111) and use your own knowledge. 'The government introduced charges to the NHS because the system was too expensive.' How far do the sources support this statement? Use details from the sources and your own knowledge to explain your answer. (Remember how to answer this type of question? For guidance, see pages 96–98.)*

Revision activities

Key Topic 1: The impact of the Depression 1931–39

Chapter 1 The growth of unemployment and the government response

1. Are the following statements true or false?

	True	False
The motor vehicle industry was one of the declining old industries.		
By 1932 there were 3 million people out of work in Britain.		
The Depression was mainly caused by the Wall Street Crash.		
The worst hit industry was coalmining.		
The highest unemployment was in the South-East.		

2. Write three words to summarise each of the following measures brought in by the National Government in the 1930s to deal with unemployment.

- Special Areas Act
- Import Duties Act
- Exchange Equalisation Act

Chapter 2 The experience of the unemployed

1. Prioritise the following effects of unemployment in order, from the worst in the centre, to the least significant on the outside.

- Poverty
- Diet
- Health
- Psychological

2. The following answer has been written by a student who has not revised thoroughly. Make a copy of the answer, replacing the factual errors.

The National Government introduced the 'Means Test' in 1936. This meant that after nine months on unemployment benefit, people went on the 'dole'. Before they could receive the dole, people had to have their houses inspected and all of their savings and possessions checked. This was the 'Means Test'. It was carried out by officials from Public Assurance Companies (PACs), which had been set up in 1928. A family could keep their possessions, such as furniture, if they wanted to go on getting benefits. If a family had any other sources of income, such as a part-time job, or the pension of an elderly relative, the amounts were added to the weekly payments.

Chapter 3 The Jarrow Crusade

1. Which of the statements best sums up the impact of the Jarrow Crusade? Give reasons for your decision.

- It had no effect on the plight of the unemployed.
- It had a great effect on the plight of the unemployed.
- It had some effect on the plight of the unemployed.

2. Group the following sentences together.
a. The government was suspicious of the National Unemployed Workers' Movement.
b. The worst affected town during the Depression was Jarrow.
i. This was because at one point unemployment reached 80 per cent.
ii. This was because it was led by a communist called Will Hannington.

Key Topic 2: Britain alone

Chapter 4 The British Expeditionary Force (BEF), Dunkirk and Churchill

1. Explain in no more than one sentence what you know about the following:
   - The 'Phoney War'
   - The BEF
   - Operation Dynamo
   - Operation Sealion

2. 'Winston Churchill's speeches inspired the British people.' Write a paragraph explaining why you agree with the statement.

Chapter 5 The Battle of Britain

1. Place the following events that occurred during the Battle of Britain in chronological order.
   - The *Luftwaffe* loses 56 planes.
   - Goering issues Eagle Day.
   - Hitler calls off Operation Sealion.
   - The *Luftwaffe* diverts its attacks to London.
   - The RAF reserves are very low.

2. Using the following words, fill in the gaps in this account of the reasons for British success in the Battle of Britain.

   Goering Spitfire weaknesses sector Dowding strengths radar

   The main reasons for the British victory were the .... of the *Luftwaffe* and the .... of the RAF. The overall RAF commander .... was far more effective than the *Luftwaffe* leader .... The RAF fighter plane the .... was superior to its German counterpart. In addition, the British had a very good early warning system known as .... whose nerve centre was in the .... stations.

Chapter 6 The Blitz

1. Briefly explain the following features of the Blitz:
   - The blackout
   - The V-1 and V-2
   - The Anderson shelter
   - The London Underground
   - The attack on Coventry

2. Read the following questions and select the correct answer.

   a: In which year did the Blitz begin?

A	1939	B	1940
C	1941	D	1942

   b: Which of the following was the name of an air raid shelter?

A	Churchill	B	Chamberlain
C	Anderson	D	Beveridge

   c: What was the LDV?

A	Air raid wardens	B	Women volunteers
C	Blackout regulations	D	The Home Guard

   d: What did the V in V-1 and V-2 stand for?

A	Vendetta	B	Vengeance
C	Victory	D	Valiant

   e: In what year was the first V-1 bomb fired at London?

A	1942	B	1943
C	1944	D	1945

   f: Which city centre was badly damaged by the Blitz on 14 November 1940?

A	Coventry	B	Manchester
C	Liverpool	D	Birmingham

Key Topic 3: Britain at war

Chapter 7 The role of government, food supplies and rationing

1. Explain why the following were important in Britain during the Second World War:

   • Emergency Powers (Defence) Act 1939
   • Censorship
   • The radio
   • Merchant ships
   • Rationing

2. 'Rationing was a success in Britain during the war.' Write two paragraphs explaining why you agree with this statement.

Chapter 8 The changing role of women

1. What do the following initials stand for?

   • ATS
   • WRNS
   • WAAF
   • WVS

2. Give two examples of:

   • Progress made by women after 1945
   • Lack of progress by women after 1945

Chapter 9 D-Day and the defeat of Germany

1. Below is part of a mind map showing the reasons why the D-Day landings were successful.

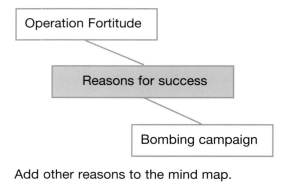

   Add other reasons to the mind map.

   Show and explain links between at least two reasons.

2. Make a copy of the following table and decide the importance of each of the following in the defeat of Germany.

	Of little importance	Quite important	Important	Very important
Military production				
The war at sea				
The Eastern Front				
The Battle of the Bulge				

Key Topic 4: Labour in power 1945–51

Chapter 10 Labour comes to power

1. Make a copy of the following table and decide the importance of each of the following in the 1945 general election campaign.

	Of little importance	Quite important	Important	Very important
The role of Churchill				
The Labour Party manifesto				
The Beveridge Report				
Evacuation				

2. Explain, in no more than a sentence, what you know about the following:

   caretaker administration, coalition government, manifesto, 'Never again', Gestapo Speech, first-past-the-post

Chapter 11 Responding to the Beveridge Report: the attack on 'want'

1. The Beveridge Report mentioned the 'Five Giants'. Copy the table below and give a definition of each of the giants.

Want	
Disease	
Ignorance	
Squalor	
Idleness	

2. The following account of the work of the Labour government is by a student who has not revised thoroughly. Re-write the account, correcting any errors.

   Labour followed the Beveridge Report, which was published in 1945 and introduced the Education Act that year which raised the school leaving age to 16. Labour then introduced old age pensions for the first time and men and women got a pension when they were 60. A family allowance of £1 for each child helped a great deal and medical treatment and prescriptions were free. The welfare state was called 'cradle to the tomb'.

Chapter 12 The National Health Service

1. Explain, in no more than a sentence, what you know about each of the following:

   - British Medical Association
   - Aneurin Bevan
   - Emergency Medical Service
   - Prescription charges in 1951

2. Choose one of the following interpretations of the National Health Service and write a paragraph justifying the statement:

   - The National Health Service was a complete success when it was introduced.
   - The National Health Service was not planned carefully when it was introduced.

Glossary

Air raid shelter A shelter used to protect civilians from air raids

Air raid warden A civilian who sounded sirens warning people about air raids and patrolled the streets during air raids

Amalgamation The joining together of two or more organisations to form one larger organisation

Beveridge Report A report published in 1942 that formed the basis of social security legislation and the welfare state after the war

Big Three The nickname given to the three leaders, Stalin, Roosevelt and Churchill

Billet Accommodation for a soldier in civilian lodgings

Black market The illegal buying and selling of rationed goods

Blackout A period during which all lights must be turned out or concealed during an enemy air raid

Blitz The German bombing of British towns and cities

Blitzkrieg The German method of lightning warfare during the Second World War

British Expeditionary Force (BEF) The professional army sent by Britain to support France at the start of the Second World War

British Medical Association (BMA) The professional association and trade union for doctors and medical students

Caretaker administration An interim government

Censorship Official control of the media to remove any objectionable material

Civil defence The organisation and training of civilians for the protection of lives and property during and after air attacks

Coalition A temporary alliance of two or more parties to form a government

Code breaker A person who breaks enemy codes used for sending information

Communist Having to do with the economic and political theory that puts forward the idea of a classless society in which private ownership has been abolished and all means of production and subsistence belong to the community

Convoy A group of ships travelling together under escort

D-Day The first day in 1944 on which Allied forces landed in Northern France

Death rate The number of people dying as a proportion of the population per year

Depression A slump or fall in economic output leading to higher unemployment

Disarmament A reduction in the size of military forces and the number of weapons

Dispatch rider A motorcycle rider who carries and delivers official letters

Dole Unemployment benefit

Eastern Front The area of conflict in Europe during the Second World War between Germany and Russia

Evacuation The removal of people from areas of danger to elsewhere for the duration of the danger

Exports Goods or services sold abroad

First-past-the-post A voting system in which a candidate is elected by a simple majority

Five Giants Five social problems identified by William Beveridge in the Beveridge Report – want, disease, squalor, ignorance and idleness

Free trade International trade that is free of any government interference

French resistance During the Second World War, French citizens in Nazi-occupied France who fought against the Germans

General Strike A nine-day period in 1926 when workers in major industries refused to go to work

GI A US soldier (abbreviation of Government Issue)

Gold Standard The system by which the value of currency is defined in terms of gold

Great Depression A period of high unemployment that followed the 1929 Wall Street Crash

Guerrilla war A strategy of fighting by small committed groups harassing the enemy

Health insurance A means of providing help against ill health

Home Guard The British citizen army organised in 1940 to defend the UK against invasion

Import duty A tax placed on goods bought from other countries

Incendiary bomb A bomb designed to cause a fire

Infant mortality rate The number of babies who die before the age of one per 1000 of the population each year

Intelligence Military information about the enemy

Jarrow Crusade A march from Jarrow to London to petition for work

Land Army Organisation of women who did farm work during the war

Manifesto   A political party's declaration of its policies

Merchant ship   A ship carrying supplies

Minority government   A government formed by a party that does not have an overall majority of the seats in parliament

Mulberry   A floating harbour used to allow ships to berth and unload supplies after the D-Day landings

Munitions   Military weapons and equipment

National Government   A government of all political parties set up in Britain in 1931 to deal with the Depression

National Insurance   A state insurance based on weekly contributions from employers and employees providing payments to the unemployed, sick and others

Nazism   National Socialism, the doctrine of the German political party in power during the Second World War

New Deal   The measures brought in by Franklyn D. Roosevelt to deal with the Depression

Old industry   An industry such as coal, cotton or iron and steel which had developed during the industrial revolution of the eighteenth and nineteenth centuries

Partisan group   An armed resistance group in an occupied territory

Pill-box   A small fortified emplacement, usually made of reinforced concrete

Poor Law   The system by which local parishes gave assistance to the poor

Poverty line   A minimum income level for the necessities of life

Propaganda   An organised programme of publicity giving selected information to the public

Radar station   A place where radar would detect the presence of enemy aircraft by radio detection

Rationalisation   Making an industry more efficient by reducing surplus firms or workers

Raw materials   Original materials such as coal and iron ore necessary for the process of manufacture

Rearmament   The building up of armed forces and weapons

Recession   A temporary decline in the economy

Sectional interests   The groups or parties that might be directly affected by something

Sector station   A nerve centre for collecting information from radar and sending the British fighters to intercept the German planes during the Battle of Britain

Social insurance scheme   A plan whereby an individual would seek cover against illness, injury, unemployment and old age by contributing a certain amount of money each week

Socialist policy   Policy that follows the idea of socialism, which means that the state owns and controls the means of production, distribution and exchange

Sortie   A flight by a single aircraft

U-boat   German submarine

USAAF   United States of America's Air Force

Wall Street Crash   The collapse of the American stock market

War industry   An industry used to produce weapons for the military

Western Front   The area of fighting in Western Europe between Britain, France and Germany

Women's Voluntary Service   An organisation set up in 1938 that helped civilians during the Second World War especially with evacuation and emergency feeding

Index